Life's Reflective Twists

No matter what happens in the future, I will always be "Teacher Dara."

Who is Dara K. Fulton?

Dara Kirstene Fulton is an English as a Second Language (ESL) teacher, artist, and author. Although this is her first book, Dara is no stranger to writing. Since childhood, Dara has written short stories, poetry, and writings about her life's experiences. This book is based on her blog, Dara's Creative Corner, where she expresses her love for teaching ESL, writing, and personal struggles with depression. Dara's focus is the importance of reflection in coping with life's many twists and turns. She believes that everyone has a voice and the ability to express self whether vocally, written, or in art form. It is her hope that anyone who reads this book will be inspired to express self, and to know that no bad circumstance lasts forever.

Mr. Wind

The sun was shining bright today. The sky was blue with puffy white clouds. The dirt smelled fresh along with the dew from the green grass. "Hello Mr. Wind, I am back," I said to the sky. There was a slight breeze. Looking up at the sun burned my eyes yet I didn't mind. I loved the warmth on my face. There was a pile of sticks near the fence. Some were too big to play with so I played with the smaller ones. "Thank you for bringing me sticks today Mr. Wind!" How excited I was that what I asked for I actually received.

Mama's backyard was filled with sticks, smooth rocks, and slabs of slate, weeds, and many insects. I wore a dress Mama gave me; a dress she used to wear during summer months. I loved the bubble bee look to it, yellow with brown stripes and a white skirt bottom. It was sleeveless. I would stand in the middle of the yard and spun around until I got dizzy. I laughed and was amazed by how the sky was dancing with me. I thanked Mr. Wind for allowing me to just be. I was a little girl who loved nature, who loved playing in dirt, rocks, and creating stories with the weeds. Mom would scold me for getting dirty and I insisted on wearing the mud stained dress home.

Mama always took to my defense, "Leave my baby alone," she would say. Mom smiled, "But Ma…" Mama did not want to hear it and would let me wear it every time I visited her. Mom used to tell me that as a baby I would sleep pointing my fingers in the air. They would move in such a way as if I was talking to someone. Mama told Mom, "She is talking to the angels." It's amazing that throughout my life I always expressed myself using hand gestures. I was baptized Catholic, but was not raised in the church. I did, however learned about the Bible and prayer.

Prayer was always a part of our daily routine. As I got older, I learned that God is everywhere. When one speaks to the Earth, we are talking to God. When I would talk to "Mr. Wind," I was talking to God. I'm grateful that since birth I always had a connection with spirituality. I guess this is how reflection came about. It wasn't until my late twenties when I began to reflect. It has helped me in many ways. When asked, what reflection is, I did not know how to answer that until now.

What Is Reflection?

There are many ways to define reflection. There may be different perspectives of it. To me, reflection is the ability to look within self, feeling every emotion, dealing with the good and bad while trying to understand it all. Reflection is also a chance for self to look at the before, rethink things, understand the what, how and why, and decide how to move forward from it. Reflection is something I do very often. I guess it started when I got into a relationship and became confused by it. At 20, you think you know what it means to be a woman and having an adult relationship. Although you are no longer a teenager, it doesn't mean you are fully an adult either.

I thought I was a mature when I got into my first relationship. Five years into the relationship, I ended it out of fear of getting married and possibly becoming a mother. I would go to Coney Island beach in Brooklyn, NY, walk along the shoreline and pray about relationships, love, or anything I was feeling at the time. I have always had a close relationship with God, especially through nature. Talking to God has helped me face my fears, reflect on things that happened in my relationships, and better understand me.

Reflection is a process. It is not something that happens overnight. Reflection can help us overcome experiences we face when life throws us a curve ball. However, it is not always a comfortable process. Reflecting can make you upset, become angry, or cry because you are re-thinking or feeling emotions you may want to forget. Reflection can leave you with many questions, even self-doubt. A thought may cross your mind that leaves you wondering; wondering what the next step should be or to make decisions. After reflecting, I cannot count how many times I walked away feeling confused, unsure of self, or worried.

When I was laid off the first time from my ESL teaching position, I felt devastated. I reflected about the day I received a phone call from my supervisor. I was confused because the day I received the phone call, I should have been at work. It would have been the first day back to work from being on unpaid medical leave. Once I heard him say what a good employee I am, I knew something was wrong. When I heard my former supervisor in the background, I knew something was definitely wrong. The moment I heard, "We have to let you go…" I felt like my heart stopped.

When reflecting about that day, I still feel upset. I cry just as I did on that day. The only difference is I feel angry during my reflection, because I suspected the lay-off was personal. The anger comes from the fact that I could not prove my suspicion. I could not prove what my gut was telling me.

My Reflection at Brooklyn Bridge Park
Thursday, September 9, 2013

I am back at the waterfront to do my usual, reflect. I stood by my favorite spot and watched the water's current crash against the rocks. I looked up at the passing train on the Manhattan Bridge, and began reminiscing about my teaching days in Chinatown. I remembered my students, the classes I taught, and how I felt. I remembered the first time my students said, "I love you teacher," and clapped as I entered the classroom. During that time, I was walking with a cane and in a lot of pain. Their reception brought tears to my eyes as I said, "Good morning and thank you so much." I began to cry as I felt the wind picking up speed and boats passing by. I prayed and said to myself, "I really miss teaching. When I was teaching nothing else mattered. I felt alive as if I had purpose. Ever since I lost that, I feel lost." My inner voice said, "If you wanna teach, teach. You have the tools already. You know who you are and what you want to do. You just have to do it."

Nature and the Reflecting Process

Nature has been a great aid in the reflection process. I love the sun, I love water, and I love flowers. I enjoy looking up at the sky, because of its many variations. I feel the sky is God's canvass. The way the clouds form or surround the sun fascinates me. I enjoy the color change from blue to sometimes pink, purple or orange during the sunset. Even on a cloudy day, the sky can be an interesting thing to watch. I admire the sun, because its brightness and ability to warm the Earth is wonderful.

Nature and reflection can go hand in hand. When looking at the sky, for example, you may notice a single cloud. The sun is out with that one cloud near it. You may wonder why that cloud stands alone. The temperature is warm with a light breeze. As you look at the cloud, you notice it becomes smaller. The breeze becomes cooler and the sun moves in a different direction. The change in the sky may trigger a memory or a thought. That memory or thought may make you ponder on it for a bit. As you feel the breeze across your face, you are engaged with that thought where you no longer notice the cloud. It is gone. Depending on the thought, you may feel happy, melancholy, or unable to decipher the emotions felt. You are reflecting with nature. As you pay attention to the natural surroundings, you wander into thought. This may not happen for you exactly, because every one's way of reflecting is different. Your environment may be different too. However, the environment we are in at that moment of reflecting can play a role in the reflection process.

How to Reflect When Going Through Life's Trials and Tribulations?

What do you see when you walk outside? Do you see trees in a nearby park or watch the sunrise? The things we see, smell, or experience can inspire us to reflect. However, how do we do that when experiencing life's many trials? This is something I tackle with every day. When things do not go my way, it makes me feel frustrated. When tragedy or misfortune happens, feelings of despair or hopelessness increases.

Here is an example. I have been suffering with a hip condition since 2010. Originally, doctors thought it was my lower back and abdomen area that caused the pain. After several tests and physical therapy, the doctors and I knew it was something else. I had slipped on some ice earlier that year. I did not fall, but the jerking motion, I believe, caused the pain. After two hospitals, MRIs, X-rays, injections, and a slew of doctors, it was confirmed that I had tearing in my left hip. A laberal tear to be exact. Although this seemed like an easy conclusion, it took over a year to get to the bottom of things. After having three epidural injections in my lower back, it was recommended that I see a hip specialist. After he examined me, it was determined that surgery was the answer. This happened a month before I was laid off from work. With no medical insurance and no immediate surgery, I had to deal with the pain the best way possible.

This is All I Want to Do

"I am wondering if you are even listening and why I bother to tell you these things that will never make a difference…but this is all I want to do"—Billy Collins from the poem "Night Letter to the Reader"

This quote from Mr. Collins stood out for me, since I tend to care about what others think of me. I know I should only be concerned with myself, but I am not a selfish person. I do not focus on myself, instead wonder how I can be there for others. I think this health setback is a true test from God to see how I handle it, and if I will let it affect my goals. Sometimes I feel this problem may interfere in what I want to do. I worry that I may end up crippled or in a wheelchair. I know this sound drastic but it can easily happen. I pray that will not happen to me. It is not to say that I cannot have a fulfilling life if I was crippled or in a wheelchair, but I know it would affect me emotionally. Although it is a struggle being in pain most of the time or knowing any little twist or turn can cause serious consequences, this makes me more determined to work harder to live a fulfilling life.

I spent many days reflecting, writing, and trying not to lose sight on what is important, me. So how did I deal with this upsetting and very uncomfortable situation? Luckily, in 2011, I was rehired by my former agency to teach an English as a Second Language (ESL) night class. It was an intermediate level class of adult learners. It was a part-time position. Although, it was a step down from being full-time, I was happy to be working and to reunite with my students again. My goal was to focus more on conversation, discussing real issues and topics that appealed to students. This was a challenge, because I had to follow the curriculum and selected topics in the textbook. However, I would incorporate my own materials with each lesson to compliment the subject matter.

The topics we covered were issues within the workplace, discrimination, neighborhood watch, dealing with conflict, race relations, and more. Students liked it and it allowed me to bring awareness to things that make most of us uncomfortable. This gained students' self-confidence. I have always told my students "Try your best." Unfortunately, my back to work experience was short-lived.

The Importance of Standing Tall

As a teacher, I educate the world, as a writer I express my creativity, as an individual I am full of love.

That same year, another lay off occurred. Once again, I was back to losing a job that I loved. The only difference it was a citywide budget cut. This affected all agencies that offered adult literacy programs. My students took the news harder than I did. "Why is this happening teacher?" one student asked. "I don't understand," another said. I still remember their facial expressions.

One student was concerned that she would not be able to continue learning English since most programs didn't offer intermediate ESL classes. I felt worse knowing I had no answers for them. I think the one question that almost brought me to tears was, "What's going to happen to you teacher?" All I could say was, "I really don't know." Throughout this sad time, I continued writing. There were times I did not know what to say because I was too upset to write, "I'm upset." I knew I had to find inspiration to keep going.

Finding Inspiration

I love taking pictures and gain inspiration through things I see. It also influences me to write. Through pictures, colors, the warmth of the sun, all of these things makes my imagination soar. I am grateful for life. Every day I wake up, I know it gives me another chance to experience something new, gain more inspiration, more reasons to write. Whatever it is that makes you happy, do it. Don't let anyone steal your joy. Different things inspire us all. Let that inspiration create a path, and experience the journey along the way.

Change can be a coping mechanism during the difficult times. Reflecting on change is both helpful and challenging, since change comes with newness. It is also a way to step out of your comfort zone. Teaching is my comfort zone. So is going to school and learning new things. I know learning is universal and will be a part of me throughout my life. However, being an employed teacher can pose some challenges. With budget cuts always an occurrence, finding a job as an ESL teacher is still not easy.

During my brief return to work in 2011, my hip condition became worse. I still didn't have health insurance, and my part time salary couldn't afford the surgery I needed. Despite that, I enjoyed the class I taught. On the last day of class, I told my students to always **stand tall**, and never give up on their dreams. I felt like a hypocrite, because I felt like I was giving up on them. I attended advocacy rallies to prevent the budget cuts from happening. I wrote letters and attended city council meetings all to no avail. I realize that one person cannot change a system that is

11

already in place. However, I do believe one voice can make a difference. I hope mines did in some form or fashion. Either way, I felt I failed my students. Thankfully, they didn't feel the same. Instead, they hugged and thanked me for teaching them. I am honored by their kindness and love.

Throughout my teaching experiences, my students have taught me the importance of being true to self, and that it is okay to make mistakes. They have helped me become a better teacher, a better person. This journey has had its challenges, and at times, I didn't feel confident in my teaching style or in myself. However, I am not a quitter and my students helped me to keep going. If I could see each person I have taught again, I would say, "Thank you for making me the woman I am today."

Teaching and How It Found Me

Before I was "Teacher Dara," I was a college writing tutor at New York City College of Technology (City Tech). I was in my last year finishing my Associates in Liberal Arts degree, and wanted to earn some money. All students had to take an exam called the CUNY Proficiency Exam (CPE). It was mandatory for students to take and pass in order to graduate. Students who failed the CPE only had two more times to take it again. If they still did not pass, they would not graduate. I was concerned, because I do not consider myself a great test taker. I was not happy during that time. I was not happy for many reasons.

After graduating from Environmental Studies high school in 1999, I was accepted to the University of Colorado at Boulder (CU-Boulder). I went there for three weeks and returned home. Despite Colorado's beautiful mountains, I faced a lot of prejudice and racism. I felt like an outsider. I met a couple of nice girls who tried to make me feel welcome. Sadly, I did not feel comfortable. This was my first time moving to a campus in an affluent and predominate White community.

In my English class, we all had to sit in a circle for an "introduce yourself" exercise. The students moved their seats away from mine. A middle-aged man, who looked like a biker from his attire, didn't move his seat. In fact, he sat closer to me and smiled at me. I felt shy and avoided eye contact with him. The assignment was to find a partner and create a mask using molding material. The purpose was to create your inner self and share it with your classmate. The biker guy and I were partners. He was nice, although his buff exterior intimidated me. After the assignment, he spoke to me after class. He mentioned the students pulling their seats away from me. I asked him why they did that. He said, "Come with me, let me tell you something." We walked on campus where he explained the racial difference and how majority of the black students were off campus.

"You are lucky they chose you to live here." I felt uncomfortable when he said that, but it did explain why I felt ostracized. The dormitory I was assigned to were for students who had high grade point averages (GPA) from high school. It was like an honors dormitory so to speak. As we talked, he suggested that I think about whether or not the school was a right fit for me. I agreed with him. At 18, I was so unsure about what I wanted. I missed being home and missed being around familiar territory. This was also my first experience dealing with prejudice.

During my last week at CU-Boulder, I told my biker friend I needed to go to the bank. I wanted to withdraw my remaining balance, close the checking account, and to buy a one-way ticket home. He agreed to take me there except it was off campus. As we walked to the parking lot, he said, "Hop on." I looked surprised and said, "Hop on where, this?" It was a motorcycle. He laughed saying yes, and I instantly became nervous.

"I never been on one of these before, I'm nervous." He got on and said, "There's nothing to be nervous about. Just hold on to me." I got on and wrapped my arms around his waist. He said, "You wanna get there don't you? Relax," as he started the engine. Before I knew it, we were on the highway. I have never felt so scared. Cars were going by as I felt every bump on the road. My friend asked me not to squeeze so tight and to lean as we made turns. I was terrified! However, heading back I felt comfortable and enjoyed the ride. We made it back to campus in one peace. I thanked him and we hugged. "Best of luck to you Dara," he said. That was the last time I saw him. I will never forget what he did for me.

After I returned home, I found a part-time job as a court reporter. By 2000, I enrolled at Queensborough Community College (QCC). I didn't feel comfortable because, I did not know anyone. Also, getting there was a long commute from home. I choose QCC, because they offered geology classes. I always wanted to become a geologist since childhood. That summer, I was accepted to a geology internship at

Georgia State University. It was a two-month program. I really enjoyed it. However, one of the professors saw my transcript and said I may want to reconsider pursuing geology. Since my math scores weren't high, he felt that would hinder me from doing well in the major. I understood what he said, but felt insulted that he didn't believe in me. I felt he judged my fate based on some math scores. "I could improve, I can still be a geologist," I thought to myself. When I tried to ask if I could improve, he suggested that I look into another major. My confidence dropped significantly. After the internship, I was in my third semester at QCC. I dropped out before I finished the term. I didn't tell my parents until weeks later. They were understandably disappointed. I was disappointed in myself.

In 2003, I decided to return to college. I enrolled at New York City College of Technology. I majored in liberal arts. I ended up completing an extra year since most of my previous class credits did not transfer. Although, I was back in school, I felt like I was starting over. I didn't feel happy. I felt being a liberal arts major was a step down from being a geology major. I lost my confidence, which made me introverted. I wouldn't tell friends where I attended school or my major.

Eventually, I decided to do something that could possibly help me feel better. I applied to be a writing tutor. At the time, there was a strong need for tutors since many students were taking the CUNY Proficiency Exam (CPE). I had already taken mine. I remembered how difficult and time consuming the CPE exam was, a total of three hours. It was two hours of reading professional journal excerpts and writing an analysis of each. The last hour was solving math problems. I hated that part. It is no secret that I don't like math, and I am not good at it. I did feel confident in the first part of the exam. The test was in the auditorium, which was right above the subway station. We had to use flimsy lap tablets that would shake each time a train entered or left the station. Between that and me feeling sick, it was difficult to concentrate.

Two months after taking the exam, some of my classmates received their CPE results. One of my classmates told me he passed, and that I should check my results online. I rushed to the computer lab, logged onto my student account, and saw "CPE exam, passed" next to my name. I felt so elated that I shouted "yes" disturbing the other students. When I told my classmate I passed, we hugged jumping up and down yelling "Yay!"

They spelled my name wrong and as a result, people called me "Dora"

I started tutoring at the writing center after passing the CPE exam. On my first day, I felt nervous and excited at the same time. I met other tutors who did not seem happy to be there. Some ignored my greetings. Despite that, I wanted to help students. Majority of the students who came to the center were English as a Second Language (ESL) freshmen or nursing students. I enjoyed tutoring the ESL students the most, because they needed help in basic writing composition. However, tutoring the nursing students was difficult. Many were very opinionated and felt their writing was good. It was also challenging because I wasn't familiar with medical terms and concepts. Sometimes, I was challenged when explaining why the way we write is different from the way we speak. Some students would say, "the teacher don't know what she's talking about, I know what I'm sayin.'"

One morning, a woman asked me to help her on her homework assignment. She was taking an advanced English class. She had to write a paper about volunteer work she had done for six months. When I read her paper, it had some misspelled words and grammatical mistakes. As I attempted to correct her paper, she stopped me saying, "I know, I know. I am an English major!" She would interrupt me several times, sucking her teeth and hiss at anything I said. Finally, she said, "I don't understand why you're telling me this," slamming her hand down hard on the table. I became impatient and irritated.

I said in a stern voice, "Ok apparently you know everything and don't need my help." She interrupted me, but I kept talking. "I understand you're frustrated but there's no need to be rude. If you're going to continue to challenge everything I say and be difficult, I'm going to ask you to leave." She looked upset and somewhat surprised. There was a short pause, although it felt longer, and she quietly said, "I'm sorry. You really think I'm being difficult?" I said to myself, "Duh" but instead responded, "Yes, but it is okay. I'm here to help you, so please let me do so ok?" She agreed and we continued our session. A couple of weeks later, she thanked me for helping her. She received a B+ on her paper. I felt relieved.

I tutored many students from different cultures, languages, majors, and writing styles. I enjoyed helping them. They reminded me that we are all students and here for a common purpose, to earn a college degree. When students came to the writing center and say "Thank you" or "If it wasn't for you, I wouldn't have passed my English class" it made my tutoring experience worthwhile. One of my classmates approached me to help him study for the CPE exam. He was a special needs student. He told me he didn't feel confident in passing the exam. He said, "I don't think I can do this Miss Dora, it's too hard and I don't read well. I'm nervous." We were at the school library. I said to him, "I understand how you feel. Believe you can do this, and no matter what, you can pass this test. I know you can and I will help you." Our conversation moved me. I would help him at the writing center, and sometimes at the school library. We worked together for a month. He took the CPE exam and passed. When he told me, I was elated. He hugged me saying, "You believed in me and I'll never forget that. Thank you so much."

I graduated on June 25, 2005 with an Associate's degree in Liberal Arts. It was a proud moment for my parents and me. I felt accomplished, because of the journey it took me to graduate. I was also proud of all the students I helped, mentored, and encouraged. Knowing I helped my fellow classmates pass their writing assignments, and the CPE exam was priceless. There are no words to describe how happy I felt. On graduation day, I marched down the aisle for me and all the students I helped.

Adult literacy tutoring

While attending City Tech, I became an adult literacy tutor with the Brooklyn Public Library. Afterschool, I volunteered to help adults learn how to read. When I started, I felt nervous. Majority of the adults were middle-aged to elder. One adult used to criticize me calling me, "too young." At every session, he would question my ability to help him. Tutors usually had 3 to 4 people in a group. I had 6 to 8 adults. My group was unique, because all of the adults were at different reading levels. Some were beginner level, adults who only knew how write their name. The remaining adults could read at a fourth grade level. There was one adult in my group who did not know how to spell or write her name. English was her second language, but she was also not literate in her native language. Despite her struggle to participate in the tutoring session, I admired her determination and approach to learning.

This felt different from being a writing tutor in college, because I did not have much in common with my adult learners. Culturally, we were different too. Majority of the adults were from the Caribbean. I had to adjust in how we communicated with each other. I also tried not to take offense to being called "Yankee." Despite our differences, it felt good to tutor them in reading and phonetics. We met once a week, and for two hours, we practiced reading passages. I would pair high-beginner adults to practice reading and sounding out words, while helping low-beginner adults practice the alphabet. Although I didn't mind rotating around the square table, it was challenging to tend to every adult learner at once. Some adults felt they were not getting the attention they needed. The adult learner, who felt I was too young to tutor him, did not like working with others. He insisted to have one-to-one tutoring. When my coordinator told him that he had to participate in the group, he became irate. His disruptive behavior caused many problems. As a result, he had to leave the tutoring program.

Attendance started to decline rapidly, and eventually my group was discontinued. I stopped my volunteer service. Although I felt bad by how things ended, I learned a lot. It was my first time dealing with conflict resolution, and coping with cultural differences and behaviors. I felt good knowing that I helped adults in reading and I enjoyed the experience.

AmeriCorps and ESL

Shortly after graduating from City Tech, I joined the AmeriCorps, a national service. I applied for the English as a Second Language (ESL) teaching position. I remember going on the interview feeling positive. I enjoyed talking with the director, confidently telling her I can teach despite my lack of experience. I passed the interview and by June 2005, I was an AmeriCorps member. I taught at a middle school in Chinatown, NY. I was not familiar with Chinatown; I have only been there a few times. The first day of orientation, I was lost and ended up at the wrong place. Once I found my way to the school, I saw my director and other AmeriCorps members.

Our director spoke to us and emphasized the importance of teamwork. We were referred to as teammates. There were few "Hello" exchanges. Majority of the teammates spoke Chinese and to each other. Only a few spoke to us newbies. Many of them were returning AmeriCorps members. At the time, my director and I were the only ones who are not

Chinese. I was also the only African-American person there. By the end of the orientation, we had our class schedules. Some teammates started on a Monday while others started on a Tuesday. The times were the same, 6:30pm to 8:30pm. There were no Friday or weekend classes. My class started on a Monday.

The first day of class was chaotic. There were students standing in the lobby asking for directions to the classrooms. Some teammates were there to assist them and translate in Chinese. The security staff informed us the floor and the classrooms we could use. We were on the second floor. When I entered my classroom, I instantly felt nervous. There were thirty-five students seated, many looked unhappy. It was a level 4 intermediate class. Their previous teacher left mid-semester and I was the replacement. One of my teammates offered to teach with me because I was new. She also co-taught with the former teacher in this class. There was no textbook or lesson plans. I felt like time stood still as we both stood in front of the big classroom, smiling, while students were staring at us.

As I scanned across the room, some students looked perplexed, some were whispering pointing at us, and some looked displeased by our presence. My teammate introduced herself and welcomed the students. When it was my turn, one student yelled out, "Where is our teacher?" My stomach began to hurt. My teammate explained that their teacher left and we were taking his place. The student rolled his eyes while folding his arms, and looked away. My palms began to sweat. Luckily, my teammate had a reading activity to review with the students. As she wrote some vocabulary words on the board, I stood stoically not sure what to say or do. One student pointed at me gigging, while another began playing with her cell phone. I eventually excused myself and went to the bathroom. I washed my hands and looked at the smudgy mirror. I thought to myself, "What am I doing here? Maybe this is a mistake."

When class was over, I felt a sigh of relief. My teammate was nice and said I did a good job. "Good job? I stood frozen the whole time! What is she talking about?" I thought to myself. I thanked her and she said she would work with me on lesson planning. We worked together for the next month. I liked her personality and she was the only member who didn't mind speaking to me in English. The only time I heard her speak Chinese was to translate a grammar point in class. Eventually, she was assigned to her own class. The first time I had to teach by myself, I felt alone and doubtful. I was not sure if I could get through the lesson. The students did not make it easy for me.

After my teammate left, students began showing up to class late. Many would answer their phones in class, and play games with each other. It felt like a recreation center than a class. When I asked them to pay attention, some students would wave their hand at me or say "Yeah yeah" and ignore my request. I decided I needed to set some ground rules. "Excuse me class, I need to talk to you," I said. I took a chair and sat in the middle of the classroom. It took a while for the students to be quiet, but when they saw me sitting there looking at them eventually they stopped.

"Hello, my name is Dara Fulton and I am your teacher. I am here to help you learn English." The student who asked about their former teacher on the first day of class looked annoyed. He said abruptly, "You not my teacher!" A classmate sitting next to him gestured, "Stop that" but he continued. "You are not a Chinese!" he said. I felt uncomfortable but continued to speak. "I am your teacher and I am here to help you. We need to have some classroom rules. Let's talk about them together." I stood up and wrote #1 on the board. I asked, "Tell me something we shouldn't do in class." A student said, "Late." I wrote, *late* on the board and said, "Very good. We should not come to class late. What else?" As a class, we came up with six classroom rules. The students seemed comfortable participating in the activity. The student, who challenged me, refused to participate and sat with his arms folded.

After that first lesson, I began to feel comfortable teaching. I knew how to lesson plan. I learned more about students' needs through in-classroom assignments and homework. Eventually, my teammates and I developed a curriculum for our classes. Our director oversaw the development process. Once a curriculum was set, we received textbooks. My level 4 class began to flourish. Students were coming in on time, participating in classroom activities, and following the rules. Many would talk to me during our break time, or ask questions after class. I felt like a real teacher. I was beginning to enjoy the process.

However.

The student who always sat with his arms folded did not adjust to my teaching style well. Occasionally, he would make comments about his former teacher being "better," and tell me he did not like me. Whenever I explained something in class, he would say, "How do you know that?" When I answered his question, he would smirk and say, "You don't know." Sometimes, I did not know how to respond to him, and would ignore his comments. I remember the first time I misspelled a word, he yelled, "That's not how you spell it!" I responded, "Oh, thank you for letting me know. How do I spell it?" He gave me this look as if he wanted to call me "stupid." He said, "You're the teacher, you should know everything." I felt amused by his response. "Actually, I don't know everything. Teachers are like students; we learn and make mistakes too. So tell me, how do I spell it?" Some of his classmates smiled and nodded their head in agreement. He looked aggravated and said nothing. One student attempted to spell the word, and then another. Then another student asked to write the word on the board. She spelled it correctly and everyone (except for that student) applauded her.

I stayed with the AmeriCorps for two years. During that time, I created two classes, a level 5 high intermediate class, and a level 6 advanced conversation class. That same student who challenged me in my level 4 class attended both the level 5 and 6 classes. He continued to challenge me, but did so in a respectable manner. I appreciated it, because I felt like he kept me on my toes. He no longer intimated me. I was not offended by his questions. He stopped saying, "You're not a Chinese," and began calling me, "Teacher." I learned to have fun in the teaching process. I welcomed feedback, good or bad, and worked harder to make sure they understood the language. While teaching, I became a coordinator and conducted teacher trainings to current and incoming teachers. AmeriCorps membership increased and became more diverse over time. Some classes I taught alone, while others I co-taught with members.

By the end of each semester, I would throw a party for my class. I bought gifts, usually notebooks and pens, and printed out certificates of achievement with students' names on it. Students would cook and bring food from home, or buy food from a restaurant. I usually brought dessert. Those were always happy times, because I presented the certificates and gifts to each student congratulating them for completing the semester. The response from our parties were so positive that other teachers began doing the same for their students. The celebrating did not stop there. As a staff, we would go out to dinner and congratulate ourselves for a job well done. On the last day of being an AmeriCorps member, I thanked my students for allowing me to be their teacher. That student, who kept me on my toes, walked up to me, extended his hand and said, "Thank you for being a good teacher." I was touched. I smiled fighting back tears and said, "You're welcome."

In December 2006, I began working for a non-profit agency as an ESL teacher. I was still in Chinatown, and the agency was predominately Chinese. I started as a part-time teacher where I taught two classes, a level 1 low beginner class, and a level 2 beginner class. The level 2 class was from 9:30am to 12:30pm, and the level 1 class was from 1:30pm to 4:30pm. I enjoyed teaching both classes, even though I had more experience with higher-level classes. I remember my first day. I wore a dark green button down blouse with black pants. I wore *Curve for women* perfume and had a curly weave (which I ended up hating, because it made me look like I had a bird's nest on my head!) The classroom was huge with bright lights and big windows. The students in my morning class were friendly and eager to learn. "This is going to be fun," I said to myself. However, my afternoon class was different. Many students were shy and did not give any eye contact. I later found out from my supervisor that many of the students had just arrived to the United States. I felt empathy for them. I could not imagine being in a new country and unable to speak the language. In the AmeriCorps, many of the students have lived in the U.S. for years. It did not make learning English easier, but they had adjusted to American lifestyle. For these level 1 students, that was not the case.

The semester was a slow start for both classes and for me as well. Unlike my AmeriCorps experience, I was well prepared in knowing what lessons to teach, had an assigned textbook, and a curriculum to follow. The slow start was getting to know students' prior knowledge of English, their needs, and interests. We always started class with a greeting, such as, *good morning* or *good afternoon*. Then, I would ask each student to say the greeting to a classmate sitting next to him or her. I felt that was a good icebreaker to help students feel more comfortable speaking in class. I would write on the whiteboard, *how are you feeling today?* Then, I drew facial expressions each representing the emotion. I also wrote the adjective of that emotion. For example, when I asked a student, "How do you feel today?" the student would say, "Happy" and point to the happy face. Students practiced saying this to their classmates. Some would mimic the facial expression when they say, "I feel mad," or "I feel so-so." For some reason, when someone said, "I feel tired" everyone would repeat the same thing and start laughing.

The lessons varied day to day. I had a syllabus to follow that included grammar exercises, conversation and listening scenarios, and reading and writing activities. Students received homework every day.

Before every class, we reviewed the homework assignment. Each lesson focused on real life issues ranging from shopping at a supermarket to asking for directions. We used two separate textbooks for each class. One was a grammar book called **Basic English Grammar** and **Lifelines: Coping Skills in English**, for conversation and listening practice. It was the first time I used two textbooks simultaneously in a class. I had to learn how to balance activities from both books, and not overwhelm the students or myself. Sometimes, I would include supplemental materials to make the lesson more interesting. For example, when we discussed shopping at a supermarket, I brought empty containers of food items and store circulars.

The morning class were more eager to try new activities as opposed to my afternoon class. In that class, we took a slower pace. Often times, students would reject participating in class activities especially if it involved speaking English. I always modeled the activity before assigning students to work on it together. One student would refuse to participate, and shout out comments in Chinese. Although I didn't understand what he said, I could tell it was rude by seeing the reaction on his classmates' faces. The disruptions were becoming more intense. I tried speaking to him during our break times, but he would wave his hand in anger, or turn his back to me. I spoke to my supervisor about these incidences. After class, she spoke to him privately in Chinese. She encouraged the student to try his best, and not be disrespectful to the class or to me. The next day, my supervisor informed me that the student was angry. His family abruptly moved to the US and he did not want to leave China. In addition, he felt frustrated that he could not keep up in class. She recommended that I be patient, and do pair work activities with him in class.

A week later, I could see a change in the student's behavior. He smiled more and began working with his classmates. He was still shy to speak to me in English, but I was proud of him for trying. I think his classmates were proud of him too.

I realized that student shyness can be of fear to speak English, or personal issues outside the classroom. I began to be more patient, and not take their resistance personal. When assigning pair work, I would sit next to the pair of students and listen to their conversation. I would practice with them by asking follow up questions to review new vocabulary, or grammar points. Sometimes, other students would move their chairs over to us and practice. One time, I was sitting in the middle of the classroom observing a pair of students working together. Suddenly, everyone moved his or her chairs around me. That was the start to doing group exercises by sitting in a circle, giving everyone a chance to speak English.

When the semester ended, I did not know who felt more proud, my students or me. Both classes did very well, and have improved their English skills significantly. I felt happy, because it was the first successful end to classes working at a new job. Since the AmeriCorps, I always felt it was important to celebrate students' accomplishments. We had a party. I would gave a brief speech about how proud I was of them. Then I called students' names and gave them their certificate and gift. The surprised look on their faces really touched my heart. What made the occasion more special was the celebration of Chinese New Year. The students brought various Chinese food and desserts as well as pizza. There was so much food to choose from, dumplings, roast pork, lo mein, chicken with broccoli, duck, sweet buns, cake, you name it we had it. We also had tea, coffee, soda, juice, and water. I love Chinese food, and enjoyed our time eating together. There was also music, and some of us even danced.

Despite the fun and many "thank you my teacher" comments from students, it is always a bittersweet moment in having to say goodbye. At the time, there was no guarantee of seeing the same students again. The adult literacy staff at this agency was small, and with pending budget cuts, no one knew if there would be more classes. I felt sad having to say goodbye, but happy to know I accomplished my goal in helping them learn English. That has always been my goal since serving at the AmeriCorps, and will continue to be my priority as a teacher.

New Beginnings

I opened a tote bag that had my notebook of lesson plans, pencils, markers, smiley face stickers, and copies of students' writing assignments. It was the first time I looked inside of it since the layoff. After coming home from my last day of class, I dropped the bag on the floor near my closet. I refused to look at it. I did not want to be reminded that it was over. Going through all the materials in this bag, I wiped away tears and remembered my students. I miss them very much. I miss teaching.

June 29, 2011

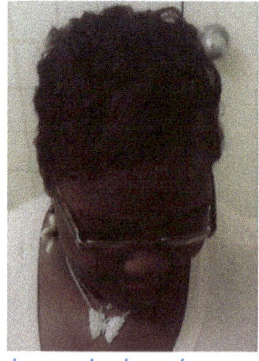

I needed a change. I went to a salon, met a hair stylist, and changed my hairstyle. When she asked what kind of hairstyle I wanted, I said, "Do whatever

you want. Color it and cut it off." Growing up, my hair
was an important aspect of me. I felt it defined me. I
didn't like my short, natural hair. I always wanted long
straight hair, because the longer and straighter it was,
the more beautiful I would feel. I did everything to my
hair. I got it permed, wore weaves, braids, and one
time tried a wig. Over time, my hair became
damaged. I did not feel more beautiful when I got
those different hairstyles. I still felt the same. I
realized that hair does not define a person. You
define you. Although I was hesitant to getting my hair
permed again, I wanted to cut it. I felt it was a way of
letting go of all the negativity and bad experiences
from the past. I wanted to start anew, and I am truly
pleased with this transformation.

Courage

Courage is something that we may not realize we
have within us. It takes guts to be brave when you are
at your weakest moment. It takes courage to embrace
change. It takes courage to look in the mirror and say,
"You can do it." It also takes courage to face your
greatest challenges. For me, just cutting off my hair
took courage. Growing up I valued having long hair. I
never had it, but longed for it. Cutting the dead hair, or
dead weight as I like to call it, helped me to think
clearer. I felt motivated to embrace newness with a
new look. Although this was a positive step, I still had
no idea where to go from there. The reality of being
unemployed loomed over my head. My hip was still
problematic, and I still needed to find a job. Most
importantly, I needed to regain my confidence. Some
days, I felt like I could do anything, and other days I
felt the opposite.

Tuesday, July 12, 2011

I read an article called, "What are you going to do with that?" from The Chronicle of Higher Education. This particular quote spoke to me. "True self-esteem means recognizing, despite everything that your upbringing has trained you to believe about yourself, that the grades you get—and the awards, and the test scores, and the trophies, and the acceptance letters—are not what defines who you are" (Deresiewicz, 2010).

In my 30 years of life, I have always felt attending school, earning degrees and awards defined me. I still feel it does in some ways. Although I like to think there is more to me than school and career, they definitely play a big role in my life. They are the things that keep me going, motivated, and determined. I have always relied on them to feel good about myself, knowing I had a bigger purpose in life than snagging a boyfriend, wearing nice clothes or being popular. Since childhood, I wanted to make a difference and school was the way. Sounds simple does it. Well, not really. Believe it or not, it was those things that held me back from having a boyfriend, wearing nice clothes, or being popular. I sacrificed those things so I can be a better person. By being better, I can be the best for others.

I realized that all of this takes courage. I don't think having courage is easy, in fact, I believe it is one of the most difficult things to possess. I am not always courageous. I think Mr. Deresiewicz said it best that true self-esteem is about recognizing self. Even at this age and new transformation, I worry. I have fears. I still feel hurt from people I care about who do not always give constructive criticism. I am learning that this is part of being human and human emotions are stronger than physical strength. I would like to believe I have courage in what I do. Of course, there is always room for improvement.

By September 2011, things have taken a turn for the worse. I had applied to another AmeriCorps program. This time it involved volunteer engagement with elders. I only served for two months when I had to leave the program. My hip pain returned but was more severe. There were times I could not move out of bed. Walking became more difficult. My left leg felt like dead weight, and sometimes I could not move it. I had to walk with a cane. I went to several specialists and had many exams to find out the source of my hip pain. I was worried.

Friday, October 21, 2011

This has been a tough few weeks. I must confess that when I am at my lowest point in life, I tend not to write about it. I think my pride gets in the way of being very open. This is unfortunate because I feel it holds me back from opening up to people. It prevents me from establishing trust. I don't like to be too vulnerable,

because I am afraid of being judged or misunderstood. Pride can be troublesome if not managed. Being sick for 3 weeks have been both physically and emotionally difficult. It has especially taken its toll emotionally. With lack of sleep and in constant pain, it makes me feel miserable. When people ask me about my condition, I do not know how to respond. I am starting to accept that I must walk with a cane. Sadly, it does not make me feel pretty. I am still worried about what will happen in the near future. Will I get better? Do I need surgery? Will I need a cane for the rest of my life? Will I lose my job, again? Will this affect my self-esteem? Will I feel confident to date? I ask myself these questions often. I don't have the answers. It just feels daunting.

I saw the hip specialist today. It seems that my hip is in worse shape than it was a year ago. My doctor's exact words were, "I'm concerned. We need to get to the bottom of this ASAP." I will need a MRI to determine if I need surgery. I have a strong feeling I will need it. The pain, however, is stuck with me until it is completely rectified. I feel I am losing a sense of self. I don't feel normal as I did before. In fact, I feel disappointed, sad, and very frustrated.

I am not where I want to be right now. I miss having purpose to go to work in the morning. I miss the smiles and warm welcome from students who looked forward to my teaching. I miss being a girlfriend. I would love to date but do not feel confident with my current situation. I do not like feeling lonely. I do not like being broke. I miss being able to take care of my bills without worrying about missing a payment. Money is something I cannot seem to have or have enough of it. Lastly, I miss Me. I miss the Dara who ignored all these things and lived life freely. She did not let anything hold her back. She always did the impossible.

I am trying to find her again.

It also takes courage to allow self to be angry while reflecting. Sometimes, I feel guilty for feeling angry towards something I cannot control. Yet, I believe this can be a healthy way in coping, and being true to self.

Quiet prejudice

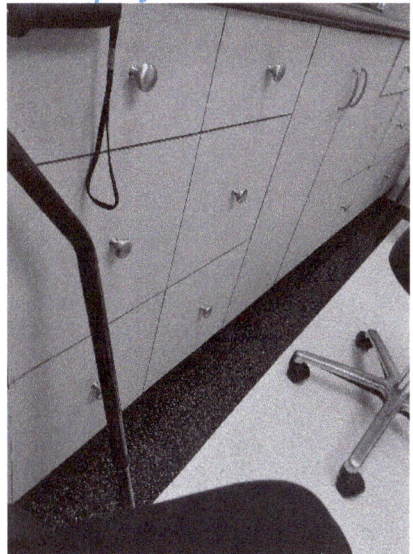

The introduction and conclusion: *Ladies and gentleman, I have a hip condition. I am overweight and I know that. I am also a human being, and endure pain, agony, and sadness especially when faced with a crisis. In this case, I am facing with a health crisis. The worst part (and many don't know this) is the response I receive from medical staff. Some just assume that I am making more out of the problem. I*

was once accused of being "mentally stressed," and needed to see a psychologist. Maybe I do, but not because I am "making more out of" what I have. The interesting part of this story is I have been to two hospitals, a dozen doctors, had two MRIs, physical therapy, X-Rays, taken multiple types of medication, and spent more time in doctor's waiting rooms than average. After going through all of that, am I still making more of what I have? MRIs do not lie. Unbeknownst to many, my condition happened from years of wear and tear, and me slipping on ice. I am not in denial. I am not afraid to admit that I am overweight, or that weight is not a contributing factor, but it isn't the cause of my condition. I am sorry to disappoint anyone who thinks otherwise.

The cane and the response: Sometimes I think society is so vain when it comes to looks. I have been walking with a cane on and off for a year, and it has been a frustrating and life-changing experience. I say "life-changing" because the cane, a tool to help one walk, has become the subject of conversation, snickering, or outburst of laughter. It can also make some people angry. For instance, I've had a woman look at me as I got on the bus and said, "Don't expect me to give you my seat!" I was surprised by her attitude and comment, because I wasn't thinking about sitting down. I just wanted to make my way to the back of the bus. Walking on the busy streets of New York City is a bigger challenge. Some people make no qualms about pushing you out the way, or cursing under their breath because you cannot walk faster. Here is my favorite, when people you know suddenly treat you differently because, as they say, "You look different." The cane and the response can be very negative. It is something I haven't adjusted to *yet. Quiet prejudice is just that, **quiet.** Yet, the impact is much louder than words.*

My Moment of Truth
Friday, December 2, 2011

I got the MRI results of my hip. Before consultation, I needed to have an X-ray done so the doctor can compare those results with the MRI. Luckily, the X-ray was done in no time, and my doctor had those results quickly. When I heard the doctor tell me the grim news, I was not surprised. He explained that I had a torn labrum in the left hip. I needed arthroscopy surgery. The surgery would be outpatient, and I could go home the same day. While in the examination room, I stared out the window with mixed emotions. Although the surgery was not major, it still scared me. I never had surgery before. I felt relieved to know that this nightmare will end, and there was a chance I could walk well again. The doctor then brought in a nurse to explain the pre-operation exams. I felt grateful to my doctor and the hospital staff for their help. The surgery was set for January 12, 2012.

The Surgery: Thursday, January 12, 2012

8:15am: I woke up feeling nervous, but was ready to get the day started. Mom, who I think was more nervous than me, didn't say much but asked how I felt. I told her that I felt quiet. Dad met us downstairs at 9:30am where we wished each other a Happy New Year. Before I got into his car, the sun peeked out of the clouds. I had to take a picture. I felt that was God's way of giving me hope. The drive to the hospital was nice, with some small talk, and Dad playing some jazz CDs. I took pictures along the way. Once we found parking near the hospital, which almost took a half hour, my legs felt weak. As we walked inside, the security guard, who was handsome and nice, pointed us to the Ambulatory Surgery area. The receptionist whom I am sure could see the nervousness on my face, smiled and said with a burst of energy, "I know why you're here! Not to worry, I've been here many times for broken bones…sports!" We laughed as I signed in and went to the waiting area. Moments later, I had to go upstairs to get my crutches. A medical staff member showed me how to use the crutches, and I practiced for a few minutes. When I arrived back to the waiting area, it was not long until I was called in. I hugged my parents and went inside as they said, "Good luck Professor." "Professor" is my nickname.

2:45pm: I was told it was after 2pm. I didn't have my watch. It felt like time stood still. I met the nurse, who was also nice, explained what would happen next. I began to cry. I promised myself I would not cry, and apologized to the nurse. She was understanding and told me that was normal. Eventually, I was sent to another waiting area where Mom and Dad could sit with me. I was scheduled to go in at 1pm, but wasn't seen until after 4pm. When I went into the surgery room, it looked like a spaceship. All the equipment and gadgets were cool to see but the operating table made me feel uncomfortable. The anesthesiologist was kind and made me laugh. I figured it would take a while for me to fall asleep. I was wrong. I remember feeling as if I was moving. I was holding on to the railing of the stretcher moaning, "Ooh this hurts," and someone said, "That's because you just had surgery." My eyes were closed. When I woke up, I felt the breathing tube in my nose.

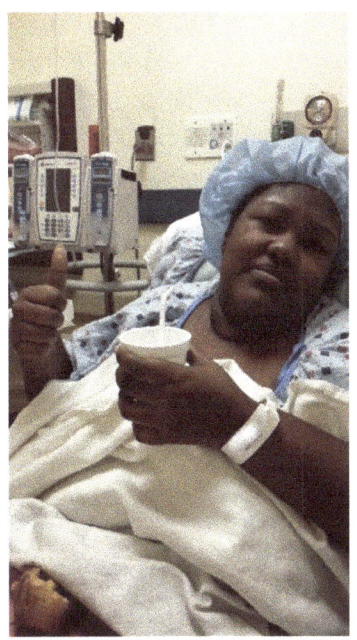

8:35pm: "Hi Mom, where's Dad? Are they preparing me for surgery?" Mom smiled over me, "They took care of that already. Dad will be right back. How are you feeling?" As fast as I tried to reply, I moaned in pain and fell back to sleep. All I remembered was seeing bright lights, and the nurse asking the level of my pain. "Ms. Fulton, from zero to ten how would you describe the pain?" I mumbled, "Eight." She gave me more medication and out I went. This lasted for a while until I felt okay enough to go home. I remember every one's voice being loud and me saying "okay" a lot. I also felt very cold. I did not remember much of the ride home, but apparently, I sent a Facebook message saying surgery went well. Getting out the car was tough; I began to cry in trying to walk with the crutches. As Mom held me saying, "It's okay baby, don't cry," Dad helped me up the stairs imitating the voice of my favorite wrestler, Bret Hart. That always made me laugh. Before I knew it, I was home with a leg brace, felt sleepy and incredibly nauseous. Mom made tea with lemon, warm bread and applesauce. I took one bite of the bread, barely touched the applesauce, and drank most of the tea. I lied down and fell asleep.

This was an interesting experience. Although the pain was no joke and recovery will take a while, I am glad the nightmare was over. I felt renewed knowing I survived this procedure. I felt God has washed away any lingering bad things that surrounded me prior to surgery. I am grateful for Him and my parents for being there with me. It meant a lot and I love them for it.

And So I Realized

After surgery, I began physical therapy. I also started meditating. I reflected on the past and decided to let it go. I made amends with people that hurt me. I forgave them. I promised myself before surgery that if I make it through, I would start anew. I didn't want the remainder of my recovery to be filled with hurt, anger, or unnecessary stress. I decided to make amends with self. I decided to forgive myself for all of my mistakes. I believe this is the first step of moving forward. It is the first step to happiness. Throughout my life, I had a hard time letting go. It is not that I enjoyed holding on to bad stuff, but I did not know how to release it and move forward. Part of that stems from childhood. I never liked being pushed away. As a child, I always tried to fit in. I always wanted acceptance from my peers. I wanted to feel loved. I didn't always get that. I was picked on for my weight, my smarts, or for just being me. I was not invited to sleepovers or parties. I was usually left out of the fun. When I got to the sixth grade, I decided to make my own friends. I created my own clique.

This clique were girls and boys who were rejected or pushed away from the popular cliques. These were the kids who stood alone in the schoolyard, the kids who were bullied and criticized. These kids became my friends. I wanted to be the one who love them and accept them as they are. We were a small group of friends. We would hangout, talk about bubble gum and our crushes. Most of them were girls with the exception of a boy who ended up becoming my best friend. I no longer felt ostracized, because I created a safe haven for me to be me.

I collected rocks. I had a big collection of rocks I picked from my neighborhood, or from my mom's co-workers that traveled around the world. I kept a journal of my collection, counting each rock, identifying those I knew and wrote notes about each one. When I reached 100 rocks in my collection, I celebrated by telling my friends, and bought my favorite candy as a reward. The boy in the group would bring plastic bags of rocks for me. I think he got a kick out of me knowing the difference between a rock and concrete. It was our special moment together. Later he revealed to me that he liked me as a girlfriend. I was flattered, but did not feel the same way. He was my friend. Although disappointed, he continued bringing me rocks. We continued talking, drawing pictures, and on occasion hangout afterschool. He ended up taking me to our sixth grade senior prom.

Even though I had my own group of friends, I did not handle hurt and rejection well especially in junior high school. One time I told a boy I liked him and he laughed saying, "I don't date fat girls." I cried. When I got a bad grade in math, a subject I hated, I felt bad I could not understand it like my classmates. When one of my best friends decided to side with the girls who bullied me, I felt betrayed. Sadly, I held on to those past hurts and did not know how to release them.

Junior high school was one of the most difficult times I ever had. Two years of hell! Being constantly bullied, witnessing many fights, losing classmates to gun violence, being robbed at gunpoint, and having low to no self-esteem, all resulted in bad consequences. I hated myself. I hated being the "fat girl," the "nerd," the "bitch." I wanted to die. During that time, I was quiet and didn't talk about what was going on. When I finally decided to tell someone, a school aide, she said if I dressed better that someone would like me. I already felt like an outcast, and hearing that remark only made me feel worse. I attempted suicide and was unsuccessful. I prayed and by the grace of God, I somehow managed to graduate from that hellhole and move on to four great years of high school.

It was in high school when I became more expressive. I joined many clubs, made friends, and loved my teachers. I went to school in Manhattan, which was great. I do not like my neighborhood and did not want to attend school there. It was nice to be in a new environment. The students were different too. Many of my classmates went to nicer junior high schools, and some attended private schools. Their mentalities were different too. It was not about having the latest clothes or speaking slang, but instead going to the park and talking about our classes. It was the first time I met people of different nationalities and cultures. I liked the diversity. For the first time, I felt accepted by my peers. People called me by my given name, *Dara*.

My English teacher, who mentored me since freshman year, motivated me to share my junior high school story in her writer's workshop class. It would be the first time I share my story to anyone. One day after school, I told her about my experiences in junior high school. During our conversation, she encouraged me to write it down. The writer's workshop class was about different writing styles, and self-expression. I had a chance to listen to moving stories from my classmates' experiences. I felt inspired to do the same. I wrote my essay and presented it to class. There was silence when I finished. Some students cried while others gave me a hug. My teacher would have us write notes about their thoughts on classmates' writing and/or stories. It was supposed to be anonymous. I received many notes that day; some of them had smiley faces on them. These notes were encouraging statements about me being beautiful, and what a great friend I am. Reading those notes made me cry. After class, some of my classmates offered to befriend me. I still have those notes today.

My teacher and those classmates have left such an impact on my life. I will forever be grateful to them.

And so I realized that letting go of the past has and continues to be a challenge. After the surgery, the layoff, and breakups, I knew I needed to focus on what is important, writing. Writing has always been my release. It has been my hope that, I believe, will inspire people. We all have a story to share.

Monday, January 30, 2012

I am learning to accept people for who they are flaws and all. I realized that being angry is a vice and something that should not be held on to for long periods. In fact, it stumps one's growth and causes bitterness instead of happiness. I would rather be happy. When I am alone, I feel that all I have are my words because I can always go to them when I need to express myself. I feel they are the universal tools in getting a message across, and can affect how others feel. I believe it can make a difference to people. All I have, all I know are my words. They are Me.

Walking to Discover Self and the Hurtful Goodbye

I like to walk. I walk to clear my mind, relax my spirit, and see new things. One of the benefits to living in New York City is the variety of neighborhoods, street art, and the people we encounter. I like visiting other boroughs, taking the subway, and learning new bus routes. Sometimes, I don't mind getting lost, because I know I can always find my way home. Walking is a reflective process. It allows you to think while enjoying the scenery. It helps me to get lost in what I see. I become creative. I love taking pictures of what I see whether it is a unique looking building, graffiti art, or a tree. I like to capture nature in its moment. That fascinates me more.

A Tuesday afternoon in 2012

When I go for a walk, I don't have a set destination. Sometimes, I don't even pay much attention to the weather. I pack a bag, put on my comfortable sneakers, and head out. I always put on a favorite song when starting my walk. Depending on my mood, it can be a club beat or a love song. I look to the sky and admire its beauty. If it is raining, I turn down my music to listen to the raindrops. When it is sunny, I like to feel the warmth on my face. I love sunny days the most. I like when it is breezy, because I can smell the perfume I am wearing. Each time I go for a walk, I wear a different scent. I love to smell good because it heightens my mood. Sometimes, my walk begins with a bus ride to a specific location, or a train ride to an unfamiliar location. If I decide to stay in my neighborhood, I take a stroll. I watch people's movements, facial expressions, or listen to passing conversations. Some of them are interesting, some I wish I did not hear. Passing by construction sites are common in my area. With new buildings developing, one gets used to all the drilling, broken pavements, and dust. There are many streets and avenues in the city. Each one has a story to tell. The types of houses or people that reside there are unique.

I like street art and see lots of it! I also like art that honors history. I like walking through parks and along waterfronts. I even like walking through subway stations. The things found in a subway station can be intriguing. The people are interesting to watch too. Their way of dress varies depending on the station's location. One can learn a lot from reading subway ads or subway art. I admire artists and musicians that share their craft with millions of people that take the subway. I love free music. Taking a walk is reflective. I always come back with new perspectives and ideas. It fuels my creatively. I am inspired by what I see.

Walking also helps in the letting go process. When I find myself reminiscing about the not-so-happy times,

I find something to distract me. It could be going to my favorite coffee shop and admiring the way the baristas make coffee. I am a huge coffee and chai latte fan. Sometimes, the smell of fresh brewed coffee or chai latte takes my mind off things. There are times when it is not that simple. During my breakups, everything reminded me of my exes. One of the biggest challenges was trying not to go to places we once visited. Sadly, everywhere I went I remembered some aspect of an ex. I hated that because I wanted to forget the hurt. Most of all, I wanted to forget them.

I had bad experiences and bad breakups with my exes. Who hasn't? It took me a long time to reflect on those experiences and the men that played a major role in them. I can say they were horrible individuals who made life difficult for me. I can say they hurt me beyond words, and that I hate the fact I ever got involved with them. That would be true. However, I would be lying if I said that I did not love them. Maybe it was the excitement of having someone interested in me. It could have been the idea of being a girlfriend for the first time, knowing what it was like to become a woman, and learning what it meant to be sexy. The thought of being kissed, having my hand held in public, being told I was beautiful, all of that excited me. However, I did not realize that came with a price. My self-esteem was tested and eventually diminished with ex number one. His mother disliked me, because I finished school and he did not. I am not the same culture as theirs, and according to her, I could never take care of him like her. What made things worse was having my ex compare me to other women, or witness him flirt with other women in front of me. As he used to say, "it is harmless."

I always felt that I was not the beauty men flocked to, and was reminded of that by his actions. After a while, I was not desirable. We could not kiss in public because someone would see us. He called it shyness. I call it denial. Behind closed doors, we were fine. I questioned why it was okay to be flirtatious in private, but publically we had to act like strangers. That is when the conversation stopped. Although he was my first, I knew I was a sexual person. I like being intimate and I wanted to express my love for him both emotionally and physically. After so many arguments and denied advances, months would go by without a single encounter. The words, "I love you" became numb and I questioned its truth.

When family members on both sides disagreed with our relationship, I rebelled and kept seeing him. He still obeyed his mom by not intervening in her verbal abuse and antics towards me. I remained quiet because that is what a good girlfriend does, right? I did not want to come in between his relationship with his mom. I was taught to respect my elders. I didn't like how she treated me, and became angry with him for not standing up for me. Soon after, a marriage proposal that I did not even know about was presented to me.

It is 2005 and we traveled to Florida for Thanksgiving holiday. Prior to this trip, I expressed that I wasn't ready to get married. I was mad at him and his mom for making a life changing decision on my behalf, without me knowing about it. I was not ready to be a wife. I barely knew what I wanted in life. I knew this relationship was taking a turn for the worse. We argued majority of our trip. I was left alone to mingle with his friend's family and friends. I did not know them, and selfishly I did not care to know them. I wanted to spend time with my boyfriend. As our trip ended, I told him I wanted to break up. I expressed that I did not want to get married. I also shared how I did not like the planned proposal without my knowledge. We returned to New York in silence. A goodbye to five years of newness, curiosity, love, confusion, and low self-esteem. We remained friends, both agreeing we could not be in a relationship anymore, at least we thought.

Two years after breaking up from my ex, I met someone. We met through social media. He found my profile, said hello, and I responded. For a few weeks, we chatted until we exchanged phone numbers and began talking on the phone. I liked his accent. He told me he is from Kenya. His emails were unique too. He impressed me by his usage of the English language. The tone of his writing style sounded Shakespearian. Every night, he would send me an email wishing me a good night, and hoped for the day we could meet. I agreed to meet him in a neighborhood in Queens. It was a bold move on my part since I never been to that particular neighborhood. We agreed to meet in front of a store near the train station. He was not there. I called him on a payphone but no answer. My first thought was to leave, but stubbornly I stayed. After thirty minutes of calling, he answered apologizing and said some workers were fixing his home. He said he would be there in five minutes. I went to a nearby Chinese takeout restaurant to wait for him.

When he walked in, I smiled as he apologized sincerely. Usually, I would be upset but his charming demeanor instantly captivated me. We shook hands and then he kissed my right hand. He offered to buy me lunch. We could have ate there, but for some reason I wanted to see his home. When he asked me if I was sure, I confidently said "yes." After our order was ready and we walked outside, he smiled at me and thanked me for waiting for him. I said "No problem." We had lunch in his room, a very small room, neat and simply decorated. He didn't have much, and I admired his efforts to make the house (which he shared with another roommate) "perfect" for me. It was a private house. His roommates shared the kitchen and bathroom. There was no living room. He and the roommates, a woman with her disabled son, had separate rooms. After lunch, we did the tell me about yourself type of conversation. Every time he smiled, I smiled. When he spoke, I blushed. Eventually, he asked if he could kiss me. I graciously accepted. I wanted him to kiss me.

I remember telling myself that I was not ready for a relationship.

Within a week, we cuddled during the sunset and woke up to the sunrise. He looked into my eyes and said he loved me. I said, "How do you know? You just met me." He smiled, "You just know. I love you Dara." I liked the way he said my name. Eventually, I said I loved him unsure if I really did. This was moving fast, I thought, but I liked what was happening. He made me feel beautiful in a way my ex did not both in public and intimately. He proudly walked hand in hand with me everywhere we went. He would kiss me passionately in front of crowds, and bragged to strangers about how much he loved me. He complimented me while I dressed and undressed in front of him. I never felt confident in my body, but he made me feel comfortable with my imperfections. In fact, he encouraged me to walk nude in front of him.

"I love seeing all of you," he would say. He sounded proud saying it, and I felt great hearing it. Once I asked him, "Where have you been all my life?" He replied, "I've been right here waiting for you," I was fascinated that he came from a world other than mine. His accent and dapper disposition excited me. I loved his language, especially when he taught me some phrases. I would sit for hours listening to stories about his childhood in Kenya. "Someday, I'll take you there Dara," he would say often. I was beginning to love him. I felt I met my soul mate.

He wanted me to be his wife. I considered it. He wanted to take me back to his country. I considered that too. He also wanted me to make him a U.S. citizen. I became concerned. Over time, he expressed this wish to be a citizen and that it was up to me to make that happen. When I hesitated, he became angry. In fact, he got angry over many things. We argued a lot, both in public and privately. When he became angry, love left the room. His angry outbursts always frightened me. Sometimes, I didn't understand why he would explode the way he did. The more I made compromises, the more he got upset. We would make up quickly after he justified his actions. I always forgave him and pretended it never happened. I did not want to lose him, because I loved him. The marriage talk would come and go. I think he knew when to bring it up; usually after making love or on a day we did not argue. Those were good days. I wished we had more of them.

One time after having one of our usual arguments, he shoved me. All I remember was shoving him back. I must have shoved him hard because I saw him stumble in front of an oncoming taxi. I heard some elder women yell, "Oh my God, are you alright?!" I remember him looking at me surprised. I stood still. I don't remember pushing him that hard. How he ended up at the curb of the sidewalk is unbeknownst to me. I blacked out. I felt embarrassed. I knew I was getting tired of him verbally putting me down. I got tired of the fighting and the make-up sex pretending that was normal. I was angry and hurt by the "You know how much I love you, can't you see that?" comments. I was tired of always having to say, "I'm sorry," when he was in the wrong. I had my flaws in this relationship too. I was passive and too submissive. I argued back when I should have walked away. He would yell and curse at me, and I did the same. Despite our problems, I helped him get two jobs. To my surprise, he did not thank me. When I brought it to his attention, he said, "You didn't get me anything. I did this all on my own. But thanks for your input." I was so angry I could have screamed. "My input?" I said angrily. "If it wasn't for me, you would still be laid up in that house doing nothing!" The argument lasted for hours. That was our usual routine, meet somewhere, talk, argue, grab dinner, and have sex. I have gotten so used to this routine that it felt normal.

One night, things went too far.

"You're hurting me, please stop!" He did not. He said, "Pleasure is pain," and kept hurting me. I eventually knew what I felt. I already knew my fate. I never told him how he made me feel that night. I went home feeling dirty. I felt taken advantage of and used. I remained quiet and tried to forget about it. The only problem was, I could not forget. I still went to work. In 2008, I was promoted as a full-time teacher and was teaching both day and night classes. Teaching helped me forget that night, and I put all my focus on helping my students. One afternoon during class, I felt faint. At first, I thought I was just tired. However, I couldn't help but feel something was wrong. I went to the doctor. Meanwhile, I avoided my boyfriend's calls. I did not want him to know how bad I was feeling. I did not want him to know what he had done to me, and what I ended up having to do.

I took a few days off from work. I went to the waterfront and prayed for forgiveness. I felt guilty, hurt, and very angry. I wanted to end my life. I cried a lot, and avoided all of his calls and invites from him. I just wanted to be left alone. My birthday arrived shortly after what happened. I was depressed. I felt I didn't deserve to live or to be happy. I hesitantly taught class on my birthday. My students from the evening class reminded me of why my birthday is special. During our break time, the students brought out bags of food and cake yelling "Surprise teacher! Happy birthday!" I could have cried standing there. Apparently, they hid everything in the back of the classroom. One student presented me with flowers and gave me a hug. They took pictures of me trying to smile while holding the flowers. I was overwhelmed with emotion that all I could do is say thank you. They saved my life that night. They gave me a reason to live.

All I ever wanted was love. I wanted to be loved and when I thought I found it, it was snatched from my soul. My heart became a victim of something I could never get back. Apart of me died that day. She would never be the same again.

It was almost two months since that horrible night. I wanted to move forward, but felt I needed closure by letting my boyfriend know how much he hurt me. We haven't officially broke up but our relationship was strained. I called him requesting we met at a public place. When we met, I explained what happened. I told him he raped me. He apologized but denied raping me. Instead, he said, "We were just having vigorous sex." Although I disagreed how he described that night, I told him I "forgave" him. I felt by forgiving him, it would allow me to move forward. He apologized that I had to go through the ordeal alone. I wanted to believe him.

A couple of weeks later, he asked to meet him during his lunch break. He handed me an envelope. "What's this?" I said. He smirked, "This should take care of things." Holding the envelope I replied, "Do you think this [money] changes things? Do you honestly think this makes a difference?" He looked at me intently, "It won't change what happened, but it's the least I could do. I am a man. I want to do my part in this situation." At that moment, I didn't know if I should slap him or curse him out. Instead, I put the envelope in my coat pocket and walked away. We did not talk for a while. Months following, we said we were going to "work things out," even though I knew it was a mistake. A mistake I still regret to this day.

It is now 2009 and our reconnection was short lived. The arguing continued. The verbal abuse manifested. The rape was a repeated discussion that was hurtful and accusatory. He kept denying it and made it seem like I was delusional. I regretted "forgiving" him. I regretted going back to him. I regretted not reporting him to the police. When he wanted to be intimate, I felt afraid of him. He would say during our lovemaking, "You know I'm the only man who would ever love you the way I do." I actually believed him, and continued being submissive. I thought that by being submissive the arguing would stop. Maybe he would love me more. How naïve was I to think that way. His anger became worse, and we argued more aggressively. I feared he would violently hurt me. After a petty argument over the phone, he cussed me. The way he did it, I knew it was time to walk away for good. We broke up and I never looked back. In retrospect, I never actually forgave him. I tried to convince myself I forgave him as a means to forget what happened. Yet, each time I remembered that night, every time he touched me or say he loved me, I felt angry. I hate him. I don't know if I could ever forgive him for what he did. I still have not forgiven myself.

Walking away is never easy, especially when love is involved. Sometimes the glitz and glamour of it can blind us to what is real. Reality, a place or state of being that isn't always well received. Love is a beautiful emotion regardless. I don't think that once you love someone, it really goes away. Certain circumstances can compromise things. That compromise leads to making difficult decisions. Should I stay or should I go? Is he worth my heart or am I wasting my time? Sometimes reflection cannot always give you the answers to such questions. Being silent may be the only thing we are left to do.

My first ex and I remained friends after our breakup. He was still my best friend, because he was always there for me when I needed him. It took a while to share what happened to me to him. I only told him about the rape. His reaction scared me; I knew he wanted to hurt my ex. When I told my friend about the breakup, he said he was happy. I knew he never stopped loving me. I never stopped loving him. We always had a strong bond, one I never wanted to lose. A year after the breakup, my friend asked me about giving our relationship a second chance. I felt hesitant. I was afraid that getting back together would ruin our friendship. I wasn't sure if I was emotionally ready to be in a relationship. Yet, with much persistence from my friend, I finally gave in. Although it was nice having a boyfriend again, it felt different this time. We were older, we both have been in different relationships, and had more expectations. He assured me that he would never hurt me the way my ex did. Our families were not thrilled by our reunion, but we did not care. We loved each other and that was all that mattered, at least I thought.

It is 2010 and we got back together that August. By September, we broke up. I received a text message from my friend saying our relationship "isn't going to work out." However, I found it odd he told me this via text instead of calling me. He always calls me when something is wrong. I did not question it, because I felt content that we were still friends. During that time, my hip condition became worse, and in October, I was on unpaid medical leave. One afternoon, my friend called and said he had something to tell me. He shared that he wanted to "try" something new. When I asked what he wanted to try, he told me he was "curious" and that I needed to accept it. I felt like I went deaf, because I could not believe what I was hearing. How could I accept my first love choosing to be something he is not? How can I accept this newfound identity? I didn't want to accept it. I asked him if he only got back with me to verify this newfound sexuality. He kept saying I needed to accept this and instead, I cursed him out. I was angry and heartbroken. I felt he used me to justify this sudden decision. There were so many questions and very little answers. I felt dirty all over again.

I was laid off from my job that November. I also learned from my doctor that I needed hip surgery. My best friend betrayed me. I felt numb. I reflected and prayed. I asked God, "Why is this happening to me? What have I done to deserve this? All I ever wanted was to be loved." I isolated myself for a while, not answering calls or social media messages. I wanted to disappear. I wanted to express my pain, but did not know how. Writing has always been my release. A friend emailed me and suggested I start a blog. I took her advice. My blog, *Dara's Creative Corner* was launched December 20, 2010. I did not know what it was going to be about; I did not even know what to write. I knew I wanted to share how I was feeling. It was then when I started to reflect on my relationships. I believe that was the start to my healing.

December 20, 2010: Dara's Creative Corner
First blog post: My Process of Moving On

I have been in the process of moving on. I am moving on from negative experiences and negative people. I took several steps to do that. I changed my number, stop communicating from certain people, and focused on making myself happy--again. Writing, prayer, music, and spending time with family and close friends, have helped me through this process. I am grateful for these things, because without them who knows where I would be now. I was unhappy in my last relationship. I felt I needed to stay to make him happy or convince myself I was happy. Although we have been friends for a long time and I loved him dearly, there were things that caused us to separate. I understood this. However, the way the breakup happened was all wrong. In addition, the revelation I received afterward was too unbearable. He broke my heart. I have had a couple of friends, at least I thought, who wished me bad or stopped speaking to me over petty disputes. I tried to make amends but sadly, they did not want to. I am a sensitive person, but not so sensitive that I cannot take negative feedback. I try to make amends with everything or anyone I deal with, because I absolutely hate conflict.

Moving on, to me, is letting go of any bad feelings towards people that hurt you. I don't want to have a life filled with nonsense, misery, or be surrounded by negativity. There is enough of that in the world.

Despite everything, I wish those individuals well. This also applies to my ex-boyfriend, because we were friends for a long time and it is sad that had to end too. I am not a hateful person, but I cannot allow anyone to mistreat me simply because someone says, "I am your friend." Some things just aren't right.

So, here I am saying "Hello new experiences and new people." It is a bit scary because it has been a while since I met new people, developed new friendships, and had new experiences. I look forward to the newness 2011 has to offer.

The First Step: Aftermath of Hip Surgery

Thursday, February 23, 2012

I went outside today. It is the first time since I had surgery. I felt excited and somewhat nervous, because I have not walked on street pavement or climbed stairs in some time. Today was spontaneous. I had to see the sun and feel the breeze. It was around 60 degrees today; there was no excuse for me not to experience such lovely and unusual weather in February. When I left my apartment and approached the stairs that is when I felt nervous. I remembered something my mom would say to me as a child, "Always put your best foot forward. If you take one step, God will put two behind you." And so I did, I put my best foot forward. I am off the crutches but walking with a cane. I took my time and made it outside.

I stood in front of my building looking up to the sky. I felt the warmth from the bright sun. I smiled and took a picture. I breathed in the cool breeze and thanked God for allowing me to be outdoors. I leaned against the building post and listened to music. It was quiet outside, not a lot of people around except for the construction workers down the block. I did not care I was enjoying the moment. I stayed there for a while and took a short walk to the store. I have to get used to walking on hard ground again, my hip and leg are still weak. I definitely need the cane. Soon I will not need it, but for now, I don't mind. I am just happy to be walking again. The things we take for granted. Something as simple as walking is a blessing. There are many who cannot walk. Reality definitely hits home. For me, I can only smile.

March 2, 2012
Dara Walks and She Is happy

"You're doing a lot better, glad to see it!" My doctor said to me as he took the stitches out from my leg.

"Wow you healed so well. Let's get you set up for physical therapy and you'll be all set." I smiled and said, "Thank you, I feel a lot better." I was done in ten minutes. My mom accompanied me to the doctor's office. I tried to convince her that she did not have to come with me. She was not trying to hear that. I am glad she was there. "You're done already?" Mom said with surprise. "Yep, told you it wouldn't be a long visit" I replied with confidence. "So what did he say?" I replied, "He said I can walk again." At this point, his assistant gave me some paperwork to review. I thanked her for helping me through this process. She is very nice. My doctor is nice too. I thank him for healing me.

Afterwards, we headed back to Brooklyn and went to our favorite diner. I had a cup of coffee. I haven't had coffee in seven weeks! Oh how I missed it. I tweeted my friends letting them know the good news. I did the same on Facebook. Their support has been wonderful. I know they are happy for me. We then went to my favorite teachers' store. That store is like a reminder as to why I became a teacher. I saw so many things I wanted, so many things I ended up buying. One of those things were four boxes of colorful chalk. I used chalk when I taught ESL classes at night. I also bought glitter. "Why are you buying glitter?" Mom asked. "You know me, I love glitter. Besides I'll probably use it to make something creative!" I said this while admiring its sparkle. Buying the chalk however was very significant for me. I want to have it so I will be prepared when I teach...again. I plan to be back in the classroom teaching ESL. My classroom door is not closed yet.

I am not a quitter. I've been told I am too passionate and stubborn when it comes to something I want. This is true. I am a determined person and don't stop until I accomplish my goals. Today I accomplished one of those goals. I left the cane at home. I wanted to see how I would feel without it. I felt fine. I went to the waterfront to reflect and relax. Although I cannot run just yet, I can walk okay. I will continue with physical therapy to strengthen my leg but otherwise I feel good. Traditionally, I always stop at Starbucks and get a caramel macchiato before heading to the waterfront. That is my favorite drink and it always makes me happy. I love being by the water. Even though it was cold and cloudy, occasionally the sun peeked out. There were few people outside but I did not mind. I had my macchiato and music.

Being laid off from my job was a devastating experience. I felt cheated and betrayed. I have always felt the reason behind the first layoff wasn't the full truth. Call it a gut feeling. The second layoff I knew was true, because many of us were let go. Sadly, the students suffered more from it, because it disrupted their learning process. I was more upset about that than losing a job. Despite everything, I had to admit to myself that the experience at that agency was not all bad. I learned a lot and met some great people along the way. I did not want to harbor any ill feelings towards anyone. I made the decision to reconnect with my former supervisor. We decided to meet for lunch at a local restaurant, known for their congee dishes in Chinatown. As I walked up to him, he smiled and gave me a hug. After the hug he said, "It's so good to see you without the cane Dara!" That meant so much, because he knew my journey. He knew how much I wanted to walk well again. I always liked his smile because it makes me smile.

Once we arrived at the restaurant, we began to have a very candid conversation. I shared my feelings about the layoff. He understood and assured me that he didn't want to see me or any of his staff go. I felt he was genuine. Afterwards, I told him that I missed teaching and wanted to volunteer as a substitute teacher. My wanting to teach again did not surprise him. He added that he has always seen me as a leader.

"You're so good at it," he said as I sat there in amazement. I am very modest. I tend not to see my strengths and rarely take credit for what I do. I appreciated the compliment. When he asked why I wanted to volunteer, I explained that it would allow me to give back to an agency that gave me a chance as a then inexperienced teacher. He thanked me for the sentiments and asked me if I wanted to come back as a paid part-time teacher. With a big smile, I said "Yes!"

The Final Level 4 Class

Saturday, March 31, 2012
"Teacher" Returns and an Unexpected Week of Surprises

"Teacher" returns. I, Dara K. Fulton better known as "Teacher" is returning to the ESL classroom! I signed the paperwork on Thursday, March 23, and my coordinator smiled saying, "Great to have you back on

board." I replied, "Thank you, it's good to be back." I am so happy and cannot stop smiling. I will be teaching a level 4 intermediate class starting April 16. How great it is to go back to doing something I love days before my 31st birthday! God is good. I look forward to a successful semester. I cannot wait to meet my new students. I have my smiley face stickers ready! Let the lesson planning begin.

April 16, 2012
Stepping Stone: The Return of Me

I feel like myself again. I am doing things differently this time around. I am a teacher for a reason. It is my passion. This is who I am.

*6:30pm: "My name is Dara Fulton, Fulton like in Fulton Street. Next time you see this street name, think of me. But if you don't wanna call me Dara, you can always call me 'Teacher.'" There was some laughter. A few students said "Teacher" when I said, "It's nice to meet all of you." I met my level 4 ESL class tonight. This is an interesting group. Not only they are eager to learn and improve their English, but also many don't live in the neighborhood of our class. Some are traveling long distances just to attend class. I am moved by their determination. It is inspiring. I promise to make this an enjoyable class experience for them. During the orientation, I discussed what I expect from the class and what they can expect from me. "There are two things I care about the most in this class," I said while writing the word **comfortable** and **try your best** on the board.*

"One of the things I've learned teaching ESL for

almost 8 years now is the importance of feeling comfortable. If you are comfortable, it will make learning English a little easier. Always try your best. I don't care if you get 100% on every test or assignment I give you, as long as you try your best that is all that matters. Teacher is still happy." I noticed a lot of nods and smiles. Many hummed in agreement. After going over the textbook and general classroom rules, I began administering the BEST Plus test. I am not a fan of this test for many reasons, but it does help to see the students' level in pronunciation, listening, and speaking skills. Based on the test results, the students are definitely at an intermediate level, some higher than others. I look forward to beginning the first lesson tomorrow. What made my night was when a student said, "I feel comfortable talking to you. I understand your meaning and you are nice. I don't feel nervous. As you say 'try your best' right?" His smile and facial expression is memorable.

Friday, April 27, 2012
The Chalkboard, My Playground

I love to write. I love to be creative. I love art. What a great way to display all of that than on a chalkboard. One of the best things about teaching is using visuals to explain something. I use visuals to explain grammar. I draw a lot so there are endless smiley faces, or pictures on the board. It really helps get the message across especially when practicing pronunciation. It is fun for them and me. I have learned early on in my teaching career that a positive attitude is necessary in order for students to learn. As I told my students two weeks ago, "If you're comfortable here [ESL class] then it makes learning English a little easier." For teachers, it allows us to *share our creativity and interest in our students' learning. In all my experiences, there is always a new challenge to overcome. I am not a grammar whiz and at times, I forget the rules. However, I am not afraid of making mistakes, because that is how one learns. My students know that "Teacher" is not afraid to have an "oops" moment, or use the dictionary to spell a word. I believe that if students see that teachers are learners as well, they will not be afraid to try. I am always proud when students come up to me and say, "I will try my best." In everything we do, we must try our best. The chalkboard allows me to display my knowledge, my art, and even my mistakes. It is my little playground, and I am happy to be able to share that with my students.*

The level 4 class were a great bunch of students from a variety of backgrounds. Through my experiences teaching ESL, my classes had students from mainland China, some from Hong Kong, Taiwan, or Southeast Asia. In each class, every adult learner has their own unique learning abilities. Each student has different educational backgrounds, work experiences, ideals, beliefs, and attitudes. This has made my job exciting. This class was unique in that they were more expressive than my other classes. They were not shy, or afraid to speak English. Many of them had worked for American companies, lived in the US for many years, or were pursuing a college education. The challenge was deciphering the students' individual needs. I tried to figure out how to connect those needs with the curriculum. I usually began my classes by asking students to share what interested them. This was my assessment to know how to present each lesson.

"Teacher, I want to improve my English so I can get a job," said one student. I drew a bubble map on the chalkboard with the question, *why do you want to learn English* in the center bubble. As students told me their answers, I write them in each surrounding bubble creating a bubble map. This is useful when brainstorming ideas, or to get a dialogue going. Many of the answers were similar, employment, housing, making a doctor's appointment, voting, becoming an American citizen, and the list goes on. I was impressed by the amount of vocabulary words students knew. I liked their enthusiasm in answering this question. One student asked me, "Teacher, will you help me speak better English?" I looked at her and said, "I will do my best as your teacher to help you speak better English." She smiled and said, "I will do my best." The phrase, *try your best* became the theme for our class.

My Last Day of Teaching ESL... For Now

Monday, June 4, 2012
"This isn't goodbye, just a see you later."

I assigned homework last Friday asking the students to write about their experience taking level 4 class. They did and shared their thoughts in tonight's class. I was moved by the "thank you "and "I love you my teacher" messages. Many said they are more confident speaking English, and feel they can now pursue their goals. One student shared that she can now speak to her son's teacher without an interpreter present. Unanimously, my students said, "We will try our best," a message I told them in the beginning of class. I was touched. Afterwards, I thanked them for sharing their comments, and expressed my appreciation. The students smiled and nodded their heads. I smiled briefly as I took a deep breath.

"I have something important to tell you. This isn't easy to say, but unfortunately this will be my last week here." As I looked across the room, I saw their faces drop; some holding their heads down, some looked surprised. I began to cry but kept talking. "Due to personal reasons, I have to go but want you to know this has nothing to do with you or anything you did. It has been my great honor to be your teacher. I appreciate you being so dedicated and come to class every night. I know it is not easy to work full time, take care of family, and come here at night just to hear me talk. I am proud of each and every one of you. I thank you for allowing me to be your teacher."

At this point, a student came up and gave me a tissue. I wiped away tears, as students remained silent. After a few minutes, one student yelled, "I will miss you!" This echoed throughout the room. I said, "I *will miss you too but this isn't a goodbye, just a see you later. We will keep in touch."*

After class, a student walked up to me smiling. Suddenly she said, "I will miss you my teacher," and hugged me. I could tell she was crying. I cried too. We exchanged emails and I told her, "I appreciate you so much; you are not only my student but my friend." She said thank you and left. The door was open. The blackboard erased. There were empty desks, and I standing alone. I remembered how many times I stood after class and reflected. This time was different. I could not control my tears from flowing. I knew this was the end. I began unplugging the radio when my co-worker walked passed and said, "Hey!" I replied, "Hey," and sniffled. He came in and said, "What's wrong, are you okay?" I told him what happened. He looked unhappy and said, "I'm sorry to hear that, what happened?" I said, "I'll tell you later" as I grabbed my things and walked out. We stood by the bus stop when I told him I'm glad we met. He shared the same sentiments and hugged me. As he left, I waited for the bus. I stood against the school's gate and reflected.

Wednesday, June 6, 2012
Try Your Best

We had a class party celebrating my students' successes, enjoying each other's company and taking many pictures. I brought my pulley bag filled with dictionaries, journals, and miscellaneous school supplies. These were gifts for my students. It was my way to show appreciation for their time and dedication. The students loved the gifts and asked me to autograph their dictionaries. One student yelled,

"Superstar!" I appreciated the compliment. They made me feel like one. The food was great, the pictures came out nice, and we all wished each other well. I did not walk away in tears that night, I walked away proud that in six years I accomplished my goal to teach English and make a difference in the community. I walked away with a smile.

At The Crossroads

Since my departure from teaching, I have been feeling melancholy. I didn't know what to do. I knew I needed to find another job. After all, unemployment can only last but so long.

Thursday, June 21, 2012
A "Hmm" Moment

Sometimes I feel I am standing in the middle of the road unsure of what direction to take. For the past few days, I have been saying "Hmm" with thoughts of where I am in life, what I am currently doing, and where I am heading. With the economy being such a mess (sorry but there's no other way to put it) and being unemployed, I have to think about taking care of myself financially. Money is something I don't like to focus on, because I do not want to lose sight on my purpose in life, which is to help others and make a difference. Of course, I need to take care of me but I do not need to be rich to do that. It is hard living in an expensive city. Rent is high, finding a job is difficult, and just to be comfortable may require two jobs and a roommate to make ends meet. I don't mind working, actually, I enjoy it. However, I would like to work a job that I like and that pays well. With the constant cutting of ESL programs throughout the city, it is hard to land a full time job as an ESL teacher. I've been asked recently, "What are you going to do now?" and I have not come up with an answer yet. All I know is to put everything in God's hands, and believe that opportunity will present itself in its due time. Despite my concerns, I am stubborn. I won't stop what I am doing. Every effort I make now will eventually pay off later.

For the next couple of months, I pursued several job opportunities mostly ESL teaching positions. I went on a few interviews where I had to do a demo lesson for the director of an ESL program. Demo lessons vary depending on what the employer is looking to see. Some demo lessons are topic specific (example, preparing for a job interview), or a grammar lesson. I tend to feel nervous doing demo lessons, because I don't know the impression I will make on the employer. My teaching style is energetic, and fun with lots of visuals. Sometimes I may do a demo lesson to a class of students, or to the employer alone. If it is with the employer, it may be that person and other staff members. They pretend to be students while evaluating my teaching style. The feedback I usually receive from employers is they like how I engage the students into the lesson. Many say I have a clear speaking voice and friendly demeanor. There are times when I don't receive any feedback. Every interview and demo lesson is a new experience. I always ask for a business card to send the interviewer a thank you note and to follow up. Usually, I know their decision within a week.

Applying for ESL jobs are easy for me, because of my work experience. However, applying for positions outside of ESL do not come as easily. I rarely get any responses. I try applying for jobs where I could transfer my skills to match their specific job position. I worked as a job developer at my last agency, and have experience handling client case files, conducting job readiness workshops, and building professional relationships with businesses. While applying for positions pertaining to job development, I realized that my resume did not highlight that experience. I did not cater my resume for jobs outside of ESL. That was my mistake. I continued looking for employment in ESL, where I became increasingly frustrated. Many of the positions were part-time. I didn't mind, because I missed teaching and wanted to be employed again. However, this did not make the journey less difficult.

Sunday, August 12, 2012
Keeping the Faith

I had a second interview this past Wednesday. I received an email from the employer on Friday stating I did not get the position. I shed a tear that evening. I took a walk on Saturday. I vented to my mom, who is my rock, and allowed nature's elements carry my thoughts into the atmosphere. It was supposed to rain that evening. Lucky for me, it did not rain. Instead, I enjoyed the sunset and took a deep breath. There is so much going on, things I want to express, but this time I rather keep them between God and I. I know He is always listening, watching over me. Only He truly understands how I feel, what my desires are, and what I am capable of doing. Not getting this job bummed me out, because for the first time I felt confident that I got the job. Usually when I go on job interviews, I am not always confident. I try not to get too excited when things look possible. When I did my demo lesson on Wednesday, I felt good afterwards. I liked how I answered the questions from the executive director; I walked out with my head held high. This position would have allowed me to teach and give back to my community. It was located in my neighborhood. I guess everything happens for a reason. I have to try harder next time. I know there is something out there for me. I have to keep my head up and keep the faith. One way or another I will make a difference in this world. I will continue to try my best.

Saturday, August 25, 2012
Turn Around, Let's Try This Again

Let's try this again. I attended another interview this week, a position that interests me. A combination of teaching ESL, job readiness, and counseling. Right up my alley. The interview went well and lasted for over an hour. I learned about a new agency and met some nice ladies. I felt confident expressing my interest in the job position. I overheard the director say to the coordinator and assistant director, "She's good." I left smiling. Even if I don't get this position, I am still grateful I had this opportunity.

I took a walk in Chinatown after my interview. I passed by the school where my ESL teaching career began. I taught ESL classes on weeknights at this school for two years. I thought about my students and wonder how they are. I wonder if some of them are still taking English classes. I remembered my co-workers, and the days we would meet after work, drink bubble tea and discuss our classes. Good times. I miss them and my students. So much has changed since 2005. It was nice passing through the neighborhood again.

Dara the Journalist?

I never liked current events. I grew up in a household where watching the news was not a choice. My dad loved the news, and made me watch it every evening. Afterwards, we would discuss the stories and events that were happening locally and nationally. "So Darie, what do you think about…?" my dad would ask. I felt I had to think quickly on my feet, since most of the time I was not paying attention. The stories about tragedies were easiest to answer. "That was so sad," or "I feel bad for the people…" I would say. When it came to politics, I tried to avoid the subject. My dad knew my motive. Somehow, he turn a story about trends into a political discussion. I always found politics to be a boring subject, and wanted no part of it. As I got older, I appreciated our discussions more. In high school, I got involved in many afterschool clubs involving the environment and animal rights. I even wrote for my school's environmental newspaper. When my dad learned of this, he would ask my opinion about those issues. After sharing my love for the Earth, recycling, and anti-fur campaigns, he tied that into politics. "If you were president and could change things, how would you change…?" he asked me. I gave my answers proudly, giving examples, and saying things that relates to politics. I liked those times together, and began growing an appreciation for the news.

"You should get into news," dad used to say after watching the evening news. "Oh dad!" I replied not taking him seriously. He was serious. I never saw myself being a journalist. I wanted to be a geologist growing up. Then I became a teacher, which is now my passion. How can I be a journalist with no experience? What would I talk or write about? Who would care? Could I do that kind of work? I came up with a simple answer, no. Yet, that all changed in 2011. I became a freelance journalist for an online newspaper called Examiner. In that same year, I met a news reporter for WPIX 11 news. His name is Greg Mocker, and he is not your average reporter. His tag line, "On the trail of something different," is a cool way he ends his reports. His creative reporting style fascinates me. He uses props, like a giant Metrocard, to emphasize the high costs commuters spend yearly to ride the subway. I like the way he takes stories that contain a lot of information and makes it interesting. I was instantly intrigued and wanted to follow his trail of something different.

In November 2010, I created a Facebook group called, The Mocker Trail Team: We are on Mocker's trail of something different. It is a group to not only pay homage to Greg Mocker but also a way for us to share things happening in our neighborhoods. The topics Mocker (as I always refer him by) discusses varies from the Metropolitan Transit Authority (MTA), potholes, broken sidewalks, misspelled street signs, and much more. He attends MTA board meetings, and talks to their representatives about public concerns. These concerns range from litter on subway platforms, crime, delays, and even rats in train cars. I admire Mocker for discussing these issues, and acknowledging our concerns on-air. On February 14, 2011, I was lucky to meet Mocker at the B63 bus stop on 5th Avenue in Sunset Park, Brooklyn. At the time, the MTA was testing out a new bus time system that would allow riders to know when their bus was arriving. I wanted to share my experience using the bus time system, and concern over the delays on the B63 bus.

"Hi Dara K. Fulton," Mocker said with a smile. In my excitement, I said hello and gave him a hug. Okay, not the most professional way in meeting a professional, but I felt that comfortable with him. It was also the first time someone called me by my full name. We were standing under the bus hub, where we talked for a while before going on camera. I liked his down-to-earth personality. He is funny also. I laughed more than I talked. When it was time to go on camera (which took a while after laughing at Mocker's jokes), he prepped me in how he would ask the questions. "Look natural and be yourself," he told me. I was so distracted by his smile, that I before I knew it we were on camera.

"Testing our real time bus information system on one line in Brooklyn. I think we need to put this on the test this MTA's grand plan with Dara Fulton who rides the bus out here. What are we waiting for?" Mocker says as I smile waving to the camera. "We're waiting for the B63 bus, going towards the downtown area of Brooklyn, and unfortunately I have to wait a very long time to get home." Mocker asked me about using the bus time system. I told him I tried it, but the only bus I saw was the one going in the opposite direction. We walked to the information posted at the bus stop and texted the number provided. It showed that the bus would arrive in two minutes. "Lucky you," I said. "Maybe they're working out the bugs 'cause they're supposed to be testing this," Mocker said as we walked back to the hub. The bus arrived on time. "You're like my good luck charm, seriously," I said as the bus pulled up. When Mocker asked for suggestions about bus time, I mentioned that the text could specify delays similar to train announcements underground. Mocker gave the cameraman a nod, and we were done.

"So how long have you been taking this bus?" Mocker asked me after finishing the report. "Not for very long. I take it going home from teaching class at night. Sometimes I'm standing here late night and alone." He looked concerned and we both agreed that the bus time system leaves room for improvement. "I want to tell you that I appreciate your support." My smile widened, as I said, "No problem. I appreciate all you do for us." I then shared my reason for starting *The Mocker Trail Team.* "This is my way to say thank you for all you do for us and our city. I wanted to start a group of people who, like myself, admire you and share things going on in our neighborhoods." I also expressed that I am happy we are friends.

"I hope to be friends with you on and off Facebook, I said shyly. "We are already friends," Mocker said smiling. I felt honored. He mentioned he had to do another story along with ours for the 10pm broadcast. I didn't want him to leave. As we said our goodbyes, Mocker turns around. "You did great," he said in a mellow tone. His eyes were intent, and his voice sounded sincere. "Thank you," I smiled waving goodbye. I watched him walk down 5th Avenue before disappearing into the crowd. I stood at the hub reflecting on what just happened. I knew this was the beginning of our friendship. It was the start of my own trail of something different.

After meeting Mocker, I felt motivated to follow in his footsteps. While still teaching ESL in the evenings, I spent time during the day searching for problems in the city. I would go out and take pictures of every pothole or broken sidewalk, and post them on the trail group page. I also read articles relating to the MTA and shared them on the trail group page and Mocker's Facebook page as well. I wanted to experience what it was like to report about problems in our city. I started with a vacant lot caused from the demolition of a church that once occupied the space.

The lot drew attention to the neighborhood, particularly to people living in my building. It was next door to our building. This gave me a chance to write a story for Examiner that was unrelated to adult literacy, a topic I wrote frequently about for the online news site.

Should I be called, "Investigator Dara?"

I have been on my own trail of something different, promoting my writing and doing some investigative work. I love to write both creatively and about newsworthy issues. Mocker has inspired me to write and investigate matters that is happening in NYC, particularly in my neighborhood. When I posted pictures of the vacant lot next to my building, it got some attention on Facebook. I wrote an article about it for Examiner, called NYC 311, and shared this with Mocker and another reporter on PIX11. Mocker reported about the lot on the news. He also got in contact with the lot's owner. I witnessed some men, which I think were the lot's owners or representatives from the realty company, assessing the trash inside the lot. The lot owner, according to Mocker, said he would have it cleaned.

After several calls and reports done on-air, cleanup of the lot began. Currently, there is a new building complex. It certainly looks better than the once dirty, empty lot.

Metropolitan Transit Authority (MTA)

The MTA offers public hearings to hear concerns about subway service from commuters, community leaders, and advocates. The meetings are free and open to the public. People can just attend, or sign up to speak. Each person has three minutes to speak about anything relating to subway issues. Another option is submitting written testimony prior to the meeting. I have never attended a public hearing. I wanted to go to one to see how it was, and to write about it for Examiner. The first one I attended was at a college in Midtown, Manhattan. MTA representatives greeted incoming guests where we showed ID, and signed an attendance sheet. One woman asked if I wanted to speak. I kindly declined stating I just wanted to listen to the meeting. She said, "Okay, maybe next time." Entering the room, I felt anxious. I kept telling myself, "You are a reporter, so report." I thought about Mocker and wondered how he felt going to such meetings. Everyone (except for MTA staff and security) was dressed casually. I dressed in business attire not knowing if there was a dress code. One MTA representative kept smiling at me, as I pulled out my notepad and cell phone. I wanted to take pictures of the meeting, as well as, write what was happening. I could imagine how I looked pulling out all my materials!

Tuesday, June 12, 2012: "Be heard"

I attended a MTA public hearing regarding a free Metrocard proposal for paratransit riders. This is my second story writing about the MTA, but my first covering their public hearing. Riders expressed concern to MTA board members about the lack of accessibility in train stations, the insensitivity received from bus drivers, and unreliable express buses in parts of Brooklyn. Testimony was open to anyone who wanted to speak. As I jotted down notes from each testimony, I felt sadness for these riders, agreeing with many of their concerns. It wasn't too long ago I was one of them. The MTA is proposing a free Metrocard to riders who use Access-a-Ride, which would allow them to take the subway free at fixed routes. Although many who spoke said the idea was "okay," many felt the bigger issue is having all subway stations and buses accessible for wheelchair bound, visually and hearing impaired riders, as well as disabled elders. This proposal plan is scheduled to begin next year. My hope is that their concerns are heard, and their needs are met.

After attending the MTA public hearing and writing my story for Examiner, I felt confident as a self-proclaimed journalist. I wanted to do more. I have been following an adult literacy advocacy group called New York City Coalition for Adult Literacy (NYCCAL), where they advocate for better funding for adult literacy programs in New York City. My former agency is a member of NYCCAL, which is how I learned about their work. There was an adult literacy rally happening at City Hall, one I have been attending every year since teaching ESL. I managed to set up an interview with one of the members of NYCCAL after the rally was over. It was my first interview.

Wednesday, June 13, 2012: "Speak up!"

Took this picture for my article, "An interview with policy analyst Kevin Douglas"

I attended the adult literacy rally to support restoring adult literacy funding. This is an important issue for both teachers and students. Seven thousand students will lose the chance to take ESL, Test Assessing Secondary Completion (TASC), (formally known as the General Education Development (GED)), and basic adult education classes because of pending budget cuts. Without adult literacy funding, there would be no free English classes for immigrant adults. There would be fewer jobs for teachers. It is a fight that we in adult education face each year. Since becoming a writer for Examiner, it has been my mission to bring adult literacy and ESL to the media forefront. This issue tends to be forgotten about. This is the first time I attended this rally without a class. Instead, I was there to cover a story. I was happy over the huge turnout. Many city council members were there to show their support.

In the midst of the crowd, I interviewed a student from a non-profit agency who expressed anger towards her GED program facing budget cuts. A coordinator from another agency told me he had to lay off his administrative staff, and his ESL program discontinued. I met policy analyst Kevin Douglas from United Neighborhood Houses, and interviewed him about his involvement in adult literacy advocacy. The crowd stretched down Broadway. Our chants of "Education is our right" were loud, and banners reading "Restore Adult Literacy Funding" were waving in unison. During the rally, it started to rain but we didn't care. The rain did not dampen our mood it increased it. The message was clear, save adult literacy programs and restore adult literacy funding.

I always wanted to visit the MTA boardroom after watching Greg Mocker's reports. I always thought it was a place for media and MTA staff to meet and discuss important issues. In my quest to learn how to be a journalist, I felt compelled to attend a MTA board meeting. These meetings are different from public hearings, because they are usually not open to the public. They are only open to media or city officials (depending on the type of meetings held). I felt that to break into the business, or at least make a name for myself, I needed to attend one of these meetings. There was only one problem. I am not affiliated with any major media outlet. I'm just a freelance writer for Examiner. I also did not have a press pass. How was I going to take advantage of this chance of a lifetime? I knew this would be my biggest challenge, yet I was more than willing to go for it despite my nervousness.

Thursday, June 21, 2012
I Made It to the Boardroom

It is not every day the public can go to MTA headquarters, especially to their boardroom. I am one of the lucky ones. Today the MTA held a public hearing on their fifth floor boardroom, the same place reporters and members of the media congregate for press conferences. The room seems so big on TV but it is actually quite small. The board members look sterner on television than they do in person; they are friendly. The MTA chairperson wasn't present at today's hearing but other board members attended. The public gave testimony about proposed projects that will improve NYC Transit. The hearing lasted from 4:30 to 6pm. As I took notes, I remembered all the reports Mocker did in the same room. I imagined him being there and wondered what he would say if he had to give testimony. I smiled at the thought. I also remembered that a year ago I wanted to have the chance to do a story about the MTA, and visit their headquarters. I am happy my wish came true.

Monday, July 23, 2012

"This is 42nd Street Grand Central..." the announcement from the 4 train as crowds of people rush on and off the train. Thankfully, I got off without being pushed. I forgot how crowded this station gets in the morning. As I exit the station, my legs begin to buckle. "Oh legs don't fail me now!" I say to myself trying to get up the stairs. My stomach is in knots while quickly walking down E42nd Street. Turning down on Madison Avenue, I felt excited that I'm attending a place where news reporters go to cover stories. A place where important people work and discuss the future of our transportation system. I am going to a MTA meeting to cover a story about transit matters. My mom said to me before leaving the house, "Dara the journalist?" I smiled anxiously saying, "Well, you never know." After being searched by police officers and having a brief conversation with the security guard, I took the elevator to the fifth floor. Well-suited security men surround the area, board members sit at the long conference table, and the MTA chairperson sits at the front looking serious. People sit around me, some with notepads in hand. Maybe they are writers like me, or people from the press.

My curiosity overwhelms me as I listen to the Chairman say, "This meeting has now come to order." For a moment, I felt like I was in a courtroom. Members began to speak while I was taking notes. I notice one of the security men looking at me. Maybe he has seen me before. This is my second time being inside the boardroom. I thought to myself, "What would I say if he asked, 'Miss, what are you doing here?'" My stomach began to knot up again. I stayed for three out of the many meetings scheduled for that day. I had a lot of notes and three booklets from each meeting I attended. Each booklet outlined the meeting's notes, along with charts, documents, and information that is foreign to an amateur like me. When it was time to leave, I headed to the ladies' room. I passed by the pressroom where I saw young professionals with laptops and cameras. I was fascinated. I couldn't wait to go home to write my article. Trying to condense all of that information into a short article wasn't easy, but it was done.

Wednesday, July 25, 2012

The expectation for today's MTA board meeting was to generate a large crowd of community residents, NYC Council members, and a lot of press. While putting on my blazer and looking in the mirror this morning, I asked myself, "Why am I going to this meeting? I am not a journalist; I don't work for the media. I'm just a freelance writer trying to get my feet in the door. I don't belong there." I then took out my makeup bag and applied on some eye shadow. Still looking in the mirror, I smiled and said to myself, "Yes Dara, you do belong there."

Going up the stairs from the 42nd Street Grand Central station my legs did not buckle. I felt less nervous and more excited. I said "Good morning" to the same security guard I saw on Monday, and to the police officers who searched me. I felt confident giving the guard my ID when he said, "You can't go to the 5th floor, it's too packed." For a moment, I lost my breath. I asked if I could just stand by and listen. He looked irritated but said I could go to the third floor instead. When I got on the elevator, I pressed floor 3.

When the floor arrived, I did not get off. Instead, I stayed on and pressed floor 5. Two nice women greeted me and said I could go inside. One of the suited security guys politely told me I couldn't stay and even apologized. I thanked him and I went to the third floor. I sat in a small room with a non-working TV. There were a few of us, some becoming frustrated. I was worried. It was minutes to 10am and I did not want to miss what was happening. I began to pray asking God to allow me to get to the fifth floor. Moments later, a woman politely asked us to come with her. Once we got to the hallway, she said, "I'm taking you to the fifth floor." I smiled and did a happy dance in my head.

The boardroom was packed with people and news camera equipment. I listened to speakers thank the MTA for restoring bus service, and offered suggestions on how to keep our system running effectively. I saw one reporter from Channel 7 news and someone who looks like a reporter from NY1. I looked for my favorite news station, PIX 11 but did not see them. It was so crowded that it was difficult to see anyone. For some reason, I felt Mocker was there. I smiled by the possibility of us being in the same room, covering the same story. The Chairman thanked board members for their hard work and expressed his dedication to providing the best service for commuters. Afterwards, I asked the nice suited security guy if I could stay for the press conference. Since I did not have a "press card", I could not attend.

A camera operator from NY1 overheard my request. While taking the elevator together, he asked if I had a press card. I told him, "No, but someday I'll have one." As we shared our interest in journalism, I asked him if he could take a picture of me in front of the MTA building. He did and I thanked him for it. He shook my hand and wished me luck in my endeavors. I didn't feel nervous anymore, in fact I felt confident. I can see myself doing this more often. My dad would be so proud of me. I am happy to have many interests and grateful to be pursuing them all, even if I am just an amateur.

A Writer's Path

I have been asked many times, "Dara, do you always know what to write about?" or, whether or not I am confident in my writing. The answer to these questions are no. When I write, I just write whatever comes to mind. Most of the time, I am listening to music which allows my thoughts to roam. That is when I begin to write, trying to capture each thought that crosses my mind. This is free writing. Free writing is the ability to write freely without limitations, grammatical corrections, or format. You just write. I like to free-write because it allows me to be honest without worrying about correcting or rephrasing anything. As far as having confidence in writing, I never thought of myself as a writer. I only started calling myself a writer when I started *Dara's Creative Corner*. However, I have been writing since childhood. I never thought I was good at it despite compliments from family and teachers. I have more of an appreciation for it today than I did before. I have a better understanding about the art of writing, and it being a skill than just a hobby. I truly love to write, because it allows me to express myself fully. I feel that my writing reveals more about me than what I share in person. I am not overly shy, but I am shy about discussing some things. Writing helps me overcome that shyness. It helps me to understand my emotions better. It helps get my point across. Despite my comfort in writing, there are times I doubt my abilities as a writer.

Friday, August 3, 2012

I have a secret I must share with you. I have a fear of rejection, for my writing that is. I realized that the thought of submitting my stories and poetry to writing contests, or publishers makes me nervous. Thoughts of what if it's not good enough comes to mind. Normally, I just go for it but nowadays I doubt myself. Instead of dwelling on it, I pray and listen to my inspirational CDs. By the next morning, I tell myself the following: "You are a writer. You write to share your creatively to the world. How will the world ever know it if you keep it all locked in? As for rejection, so what! Not everyone will like what you say or do but then again someone just might. You won't know unless you try."

When It Is Time, It Is Time

"When you open one door, there will be another one to open. It gets harder each time but if you stay focused, the doors will open for you." --My dad

My dad used to say this to me growing up. I always found it motivating and it has kept me steadfast in pursuing my goals. I appreciate his advice and for believing in me. I am opening that door dad. Wherever that door leads me, I will go through it and embrace what it has to offer. When you want something bad enough, you don't stop until you get it. Self-motivation is the key to success. I am focusing on me now and not afraid to be direct about it. I am ready to make my dreams a reality.

Sunday, September 23, 2012
Teachers Never Stop Teaching: ESL
Conversations

I am teaching again, but this time I'm doing things my way. Beginning October 14, I will be offering a free ESL conversation class at a local recreational center. Every Sunday afternoon until December 16, students

will have the chance to practice speaking English in a fun, pressure free environment. I booked a classroom from a local recreation center. Now, I just need students. I made flyers and gave them out to local businesses. I posted about my free class on Facebook and the response was great. Majority of my former students are interested and say they will attend. I look forward to seeing them again. I missed them. I miss teaching. My goal is to give back to a community that welcomed me when I first started teaching. No matter what happens in the job market, teachers never stop teaching.

My class, *ESL Conversations* was a free English class for adult immigrants. The purpose was for students to practice speaking English in a fun, pressure-free learning environment. It was also a way for them to use English in real life, daily activities. This was an intermediate level English class. We met every Saturday afternoon, and lessons were about students' interests. On the first day of class, only four students showed up. Over time, the class size grew. It was a reunion in many ways. These were former students from both my previous agency, and when I was in the AmeriCorps. It felt good seeing them again, and watching them share stories of being in "Teacher Dora's class." Although this was my first time creating and managing my own ESL program, it felt great being back in the classroom.

Social Work Beginnings

While teaching ESL at my former agency, I took a family development training course. I learned about case management and counseling clients in human services agencies. I enjoyed the training, because I learned something new, social work. I also liked it, because I was the only ESL teacher in class among social workers and case managers. It was a three-month course, and I graduated with a credential. This is helpful when applying for jobs in social services. I liked the experience so much that I decided to pursue a second Associates degree. In 2010, I was accepted into Rasmussen College's online Associates in Human Services program. I graduated in June 2011.

Since then, I became a member of the National Association of Social Workers (NASW), where I took additional training in social work. I admire the social work field, because it allows one to help and empower people in need. I like that a social worker becomes the voice for the voiceless, advocates for better social systems, and passionate about making a difference. I have always wanted to be part of a community of people who strive to help others. I love helping people, and feel social work will allow me to do that and more. That is what led me to pursue a Master's in Social Work.

Tuesday, September 25, 2012
Graduate School Acceptance and Future Social Worker

I am a graduate student. Today, I was accepted to the University of Southern California (USC) Master's in Social Work program. No, I am not moving to California (maybe I will someday). I am part of their virtual program where I will be taking the same classes, as on-campus students. This will be challenging and something I haven't done before. I spoke to my admissions advisor, and she told me this MSW program is "highly competitive." The admissions committee really liked my personal statement. I am honored, and I thank USC for accepting me into their program. I shared the good news on Facebook and Twitter and the response was overwhelming! I thank all my friends for their support and for believing in me. It means a lot, especially when beginning a new journey. A friend and social worker asked me if I was excited. I told him I was, but did not mention how nervous I feel. Social work is definitely different from teaching English. Yet, I believe there is a strong connection between the two, and want to bring them both together. I look forward to starting my classes and field placement. I hope wherever I am placed, I will gain the necessary skills needed to be a successful social worker. No matter what happens in this new journey, I will always be a teacher.

Hurricane Sandy: The Event That Changed My Life

Tuesday, October 30, 2012
Hurricane Sandy

I am lost for words tonight. The destruction Sandy has caused is unprecedented. MTA subways are shut down until further notice, there is limited bus service in all five boroughs; some bridges and tunnels remain closed as well as LaGuardia airport. People lost their homes due to flooding, fire, or uprooted trees that toppled on houses and cars. Sadly, many lives were lost. I've been watching the news coverage since Monday morning and throughout the night. My neighborhood was affected but not as bad as other areas. My heart goes out to friends who were affected by this storm. I am grateful to the first responders and volunteers who sacrificed their lives to help others. I am grateful to be here, because none of us was exempt from this storm. Times like this makes you think about the important things in life. The petty bullshit we tend to focus on, the prejudices we inflict on one another, the unnecessary hate, none of that matters when we are in the eye of a storm. We all become victims. The arrival of hurricane Sandy has humbled me and made me wiser. Nature's forces are bigger than we are. It affects us all. I signed up to volunteer in the recovery efforts of Sandy's aftermath. I pray I can be of some comfort to people whose experienced great lost.

"God is our refuge and strength, a very present help in trouble" (Psalm 46:1, The New King James Version).

ESL Conversations Class Cancelled

The recreational center, where we had class, suffered flooding from the storm. Some of my students' homes experienced the same ordeal. I decided to cancel the class until things got better. Unfortunately, I had to cancel class indefinitely. What many people don't know is I used my unemployment money to rent out the classroom. It was expensive, but considerably cheaper than what other places were charging. Shortly after the storm, my unemployment benefits stopped, and I could no longer pay rent. I was disappointed I had to cancel my class. It was my chance to prove to self that I could teach without any overhead or managerial staff. Thankfully, my students were understanding of the situation, and thanked me for teaching again. I promised them that I would do this again in the near future.

The Aftermath of Hurricane Sandy

I spent the next couple of months documenting the aftermath of hurricane Sandy, as well as working as a volunteer. I felt moved to see the devastation up close and personal. I believed that seeing it in person would make it more real. That realness made me want to help. I was also inspired to help after a friend of mine lost everything to Sandy. I needed to volunteer and I needed to be there for her.

Sunday, November 18, 2012
Post hurricane Sandy: Coney Island

I went to Coney Island today. I like to go there when I need to reflect. However, this time was different. It has been two weeks since hurricane Sandy hit NYC, and her presence is still felt throughout the boroughs. Coney Island is just one of the many badly hit areas. I saw the images of Coney Island on the news, but I wanted to see it for myself. When I got off the F train at Stillwell Ave, it was quiet. This station is always bustling with people. Very few people were around and many spoke quietly. I felt sadness while passing by the now closed stores inside the station. I quickly noticed a line along the "Coney Island" sign on a building's wall. That line is where the water rose during the hurricane. A reality of how powerful Sandy was, and the amount of flooding Coney Island endured.

I walked along the boardwalk and it felt eerie. There were people walking, bike riding, some pushing baby strollers, but overall it was quiet. Parts of the boardwalk was broken with small piles of sand, and huge shovels left on the beach. Some people were walking along the shoreline taking pictures, some stood on the boardwalk saying "wow." The sun was beautiful, as always. A sign of hope I guess. I sat by the walkway where I usually go to reflect. I can see why it is closed. I almost cried seeing how much damage left behind. I thought of the residents who live in the area. I wondered how they are coping with Sandy's aftermath. I hope life goes back to normal for them. Sadly, for some that will not be the case. Many lost their homes during this hurricane. I hope to help the victims of Sandy in one way or another.

Wednesday, December 5, 2012
Dara and Post-Sandy Relief: "I can't just sit and do nothing."

Day 1: Midland Beach, Staten Island

I signed up as a new volunteer with "Occupy Sandy," a group of volunteers who set up shop at specific locations to volunteer. They are not affiliates of any volunteer organization or government agency. They are just regular people, who believe in the human spirit and want to make a difference. The meeting place was at a local church in Brooklyn. There was a huge "Occupy Sandy" sign in front of the church. When I walked inside, there was a brief orientation about the expectations of the day. I learned the difference between **mutual aid** and **charity**. Mutual aid is the ability to make a human connection with the people you are helping. Charity is monetary donations through organizations.

The people seemed friendly, many gathering supplies to deliver to hardest hit areas such as Coney Island, Brooklyn, Far Rockaway, Queens and Staten Island. I quickly realized that despite all of us gathered at one place, we are individuals making our own decisions in how we want to help. There was no organizer or go to person for a plan of action. As I was also told, "There are no limitations, everyone is their own leader." Some of these individuals were from the Occupy Wall Street movement a year ago. It was a movement that was filled with controversy, advocacy, and lots of media attention. I couldn't help but feel a little apprehensive, hoping I didn't sign up to a radical form of helping people. I'm just a volunteer looking to make a difference. This should be interesting, I thought to myself.

A van was transporting volunteers to Staten Island and I went along for the ride. As everyone were chatting, I observed the many downed trees and houses destroyed by hurricane Sandy. There were many yellow and red signs on front doors stating if a house was habitable or not. This is Midland Beach, Staten Island. We pulled up to a food distribution *center where we were greeted by locals and organizers of the center. There were a lot of "thank you" comments and handshakes. Retired firefighters and police officers were cooking food on one side, and on the other were tents for volunteers to sign up. There was a table by the front gate where volunteers helped residents with questions, or requests for food, supplies etc.*

I helped by cleaning the office area as well as organized the food items in the "food store." This food store is a room where residents can "shop" for what they need without payment. The hardest part of the day was the lifting and distributing cases of tomato sauce into the supply room. Each of us handed the cases to the person behind us. The cases were not too heavy, but the fast pace made it feel like a workout. I think I grew extra muscles on my arms! I did not get a chance to do any canvassing around the neighborhood to check in on residents. I hope to do that next time.

I almost cried when talking to another volunteer about this hurricane. Watching people come in and sort through the cans of food, or ask questions like, "Do we need another one of these? I think we ran out," really got to me. When I saw a woman with her little boy sort through toiletries and baby items, it made me sad. She and her son looked sad. The mom kept her head down the whole time and softly said "Thank you" as she left the center. I wanted to hug her. Instead, I stood paralyzed as I watched her and her son leave. When I shared that with one of the volunteers, I could feel my eyes welling up. I took a sip of coffee.

Thursday, December 6, 2012
Day 2: Red Hook, Brooklyn

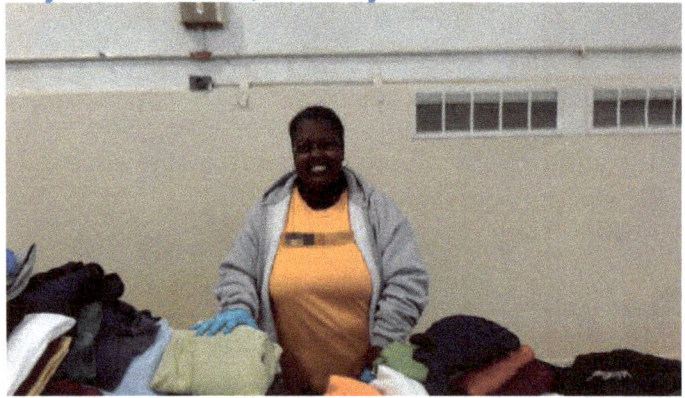

I visited a community center in Red Hook, Brooklyn. They were in need of volunteers to sort and organize donated clothes. A nice woman and man welcomed me, and showed me the gymnasium where piles of clothes were stacked high on tables. At first, it was just the three of us until two more volunteers joined in. I mostly worked on organizing the coats and sweaters by size, and re-arranging the piles of clothes. It was good to see the large amount of donations they received. Sorting these clothes was in preparation of a free flea market happening on Saturday. People can come and take any clothing they need. Majority of the clothes and coats were in good condition, a variety of men's, women's, and children's wear. There were also stuffed animals, gloves, scarfs, hats, and socks. I had nice conversations with everyone. The woman and man who greeted me shared that their offices in Coney Island were "badly damaged," and as a result, they had to move to this center. When it was time for me to leave, the woman said, "You have to go now Ms. Dora? Hope you'll come back." I felt humbled. I

104

smiled and said, "Yes, I will be back."

I met some nice people these past two days. They shared with me their Sandy experiences whether personal or job related. I am humbled by this experience, because it makes me realize how blessed I truly am. I have a warm home to go to, food to eat, clothes to wear, and people in my life who love me. To think there are so many out there who don't have these things it breaks my heart. What I saw in Staten Island and Red Hook brought me back to why I want to be a social worker. It also helped me see the impact I left on others through my actions. Having people I just met thank me for helping them is humbling and special. I thank them for allowing me to help.

Friday, December 7, 2012
Day 3: Far Rockaway, Queens

I am writing this with much sadness in my heart, and anger by what I have seen. Today, I made it to Rockaway, Queens. I was with Occupy Sandy. I needed to be there not only to see the devastation, but also to understand its impact on residents. As we drove along Cross Bay Boulevard and approached Rockaway Park, I felt anxious by what I would

possibly see. A volunteer said, "We're here," and my stomach began to hurt. We arrived at one of the hubs for supply drop-off, volunteer sign up, and outreach. As we got out of the car, I smelled a damp, burnt smell lingering in the air. I could not help but to approach the rubble near Beach 114 Street. I lost my breath for a moment. A vacant lot full of burnt debris scattered everywhere. There were rows of businesses burned down, and piles of wood and garbage along the sidewalk. A nearby train station was out of service due to burnt tracks. Similar to Coney Island, there were few people around. It was also an eerie silence. I saw one bus running, as well as, cars and some emergency/disaster relief vehicles. I took pictures trying to understand how this could have happened. I decided to make a video. While speaking on video, I felt the tears well up in my eyes. My voice cracked. Once I stopped recording, I cried. I didn't know it was this bad.

We visited different hubs throughout Rockaway driving from Beach 139 Street to Beach 38 Street. I helped load food and supplies onto a truck that will take them to another distribution center. I had an opportunity to have lunch with local residents and volunteers. I observed how residents dealt with waiting on line for lunch. Most of the volunteers serving lunch were from various volunteer organizations. I asked them how they were doing. Many told me it has been hard but happy there's "some progress." While standing on line, I felt guilty. I did not want to eat. My thought was how I could eat when so many probably haven't eaten a decent meal in weeks. I looked around and saw a massage table with pamphlets about relieving stress. Other tables had members from government agencies. There was a table dedicated for volunteer sign up. At each distribution center or hub, I spoke with local residents and volunteers, many who live in Rockaway. I think one woman said it best, "You have to find a balance. You have to remember to take care of yourself, because if you don't you won't be any good to anybody." She is a volunteer who works in trauma relief. I appreciated her words. I needed to hear that today.

We stopped at another hub at Beach 109 Street. A volunteer and I went on the beach to see Sandy's effects. In shock, I saw there was no boardwalk. "There's no boardwalk? How is that possible! I wasn't ready for this," I said to a volunteer. She nodded her head in agreement. Piles of sand dunes sat along what was once the boardwalk. The waves were crashing along the shoreline. I stood in silence. There was a pine tree sitting on the beach. A sign of hope I suppose. It had no decorations on it. Thinking about all the people who lost their homes or had property damage made me feel bad. How are they going to cope during a season that is about celebration, gift giving, and spending money? I wonder how their Christmas holiday will be.

When we returned to the main hub near Beach 114 Street, I spoke to a man whose brother lives in Rockaway. He said his brother "wasn't badly affected but was affected." I told him that he and his brother are in my prayers. He shook my hand and asked for my name. When I told him, he said "Thank you Dara." I met a volunteer who has been working in Rockaway for several weeks. He has been working on the construction and mold removal projects. We had a nice conversation about the importance of volunteering. Before I left, he gave me a hug. I said, "Awe, thanks I needed one of these. I'll never say no to a hug, I'm a hugger." We laughed and he replied, "It's no problem."

The sun began to set, and the volunteers were getting ready to head back to Brooklyn. While waiting for one volunteer, I walked back to Beach 114 Street and stood there looking at the debris. I said a prayer. I thought about my friend who lives in the area. I shed a tear for her; she is one of many that lost so much from Sandy. I hope to see her soon. When I got into the car, I sat quietly thinking about today. The things I witnessed will always be in my head. I will never forget the volunteers I met. The faces of the residents I saw throughout the day will remain in my heart. I observed a lot today. There were some volunteers who had bad attitudes and complained majority of the time. While talking to other volunteers and some residents, I learned about the not-so-charitable things happening in Rockaway. That was disheartening to hear. The limitations of what we can do are frustrating as a volunteer. I feel bad I cannot do more, because the need is greater than the cause. I will not stop helping people. If I do, then I failed as someone who cares about the community. I will be back.

After volunteering in Sandy relief, I reflected a lot. In November, I made the decision not to attend graduate school, because I wasn't sure if I was ready. However, during my time volunteering, I felt compelled to reconsider my decision. I wanted to do more. I wanted to help more people. I spoke to one of the volunteers when we were at Rockaway. I expressed my interest in social work and decision not to pursue graduate school. She seemed surprised and asked me why. When I mentioned my concerns of finances and whether I was ready for the challenge, she asked, "What made you want to volunteer here?" I told her how sad I felt by what the residents had to endure in the storm's aftermath. I also mentioned that a friend of mine lost everything to Sandy and I wanted to help. She then looked at me and said, "Well then that's your answer. You have the personality for social work. You love helping people. I say go for it."

End of Year Reflection: 2012

At the end of every year, I reflect on the events that occurred in that year. I reflect on the things I pursued and accomplished. I reflect on the people I met and those I lost. I reflect on the things I hope to change for the New Year. This was not a bad year, but definitely a reflective one. I learned a lot, especially about myself, and the events that affected my life in many ways.

Saturday, December 15, 2012
You Are Not Forgotten Dara

I haven't been feeling happy lately. Sometimes I feel my dream is fading away. The further I reach for it, the longer the distance. I have a vision as to where I want to be, and what I want to be doing. The vision has not left me; just getting there has been a challenge. I haven't consistently taught since working at my last agency. I miss the anticipation and joy I had knowing there was a class to teach. That joy put a smile on my face each day I woke up. No matter what was happening in my life during those times, I felt happy knowing there was a group of people looking forward to see me. I miss that sense of importance. Being a writer has been a journey in itself. To say I am a "writer" took some time getting used to. I always thought that to call oneself a writer meant to be a published author. I realize that is not necessarily true. To me, a writer is one who can express his or herself through written words with the ability to make it comprehensible, and effective enough to grab the reader's attention. I feel I do that through my words. That makes me a writer.

As for my quest to becoming a social worker, the journey continues. Shortly after volunteering in hurricane Sandy relief, I contacted the student advisor from the University of Southern California (USC). In my conversation with her, I shared my doubts and concern over the challenging workload, and financial responsibilities. I also expressed my reconsideration to attend rather than withdraw. The advisor was nice and understood my concerns. She offered me the chance to change my start date. I will start in January 2013. She also encouraged me to remain a student at USC, because I have worked hard to become one. When hurricane Sandy hit and I had the opportunity to volunteer in relief efforts, I grew a deeper appreciation for the field of social work. I appreciated being a Masters in Social Work (MSW) student. It was a reminder that I am capable of becoming a social worker despite the challenges that lie ahead. I feel I made the right decision.

I took a walk. It was reflective and comforting. I saw many Christmas trees in the downtown area of Brooklyn. The lights and colorful decorations always put a smile on my face. I went to my favorite diner, ate delicious food, and chatted with the staff. I had good conversation with mom and talked about why Christmas is a beautiful holiday. I bought different kinds of body sprays and lotions from a store that can make any woman feel beautiful. I smiled. It was a nice day. I look forward to more nice days ahead. I know I will feel happier, all in due time.

Monday, December 31, 2012
My Year In Review

It was just a year ago when I said, "Happy New Year" to my mom and brother. I texted this message to friends from my cell phone. I wished everyone a good new year 2012 on Facebook and Twitter. In a few more hours, I will say "Happy New Year 2013." Where does the time go? Year 2012 was a good year, especially for the Creative Corner blog. There were more views and readership this year than last. I had a chance to discuss my posts with fans of the blog, as well as, share with people who never heard of the Dara's Creative Corner. I am happy by how far this blog has come in two years. I am very proud of that. This year also changed my life. I had a successful hip surgery that allows me to walk today. I thank God every day I can walk with no assistance.

I turned 31 and gained new perspective about life. I have let go of old emotional baggage, volunteered, and pursued all my career interests. I'm grateful to be writing for Examiner, covering stories about my passion, adult literacy/ESL and the MTA. Being on TV news has been great too, allowing my voice to be heard. Having a chance to meet Greg Mocker from PIX 11 news, and attending public hearings and MTA board meetings were experiences I will never forget. I even became more creative with my writing. Writing poems about things that I was once shy about, has

boosted my ego. I am no longer afraid to speak my mind about things that are personal to me.

Late summer, I earned my Teaching English to Speakers of Other Languages (TESOL) certification and by fall, I taught my own ESL class at a recreational center. Although the class was short lived, it was a chance for me to reconnect with former students. It also showed me that I am capable of having my own class, and do things my way. During my Sandy relief volunteer experience, I became a certified client caseworker with the American Red Cross, and started volunteering shortly afterwards. Lastly, I was accepted to the University of Southern California (USC) Master's in Social Work program, which is something I cannot describe in words. I am so proud to be a MSW student and pursue a career I greatly respect.

On a personal note, I loved me more this year than last. I have become more direct and no longer tolerate any form of mistreatment. That has ended some friendships, which I do not mind. A true friend treats others the way they want to be treated. I've had some down times of feeling unappreciated in current friendships. It is easy for me to love and be there for others. Unfortunately, I went from being a supportive friend to being a people pleaser. I allowed myself to be too open; I believe for some people they felt it was okay to take advantage. I have cried to a few people that I wish I hadn't, and revealed my dreams and goals to some that displayed envy. How unfortunate. I now know that I can't be a people pleaser. It is not possible to please everyone. It is not healthy and fair to self. I will no longer expect anything from anyone. Lastly, I will stop holding on to those who don't want to be held. Letting go has never been easy for me. I care and love people very much, maybe too much. Despite how I feel, I deserve to be loved and cared for too. Friendship, like relationships, it is a two way street.

I hope this New Year will be one of peace, happiness, love, and more opportunities.

2013: A New Year and Journey as a Client Caseworker

I took a walk through Chinatown. I remember how it was when I started teaching ESL back in 2005. How different it was then. It was so crowded with locals and tourists. Restaurants and cafes were plenty on every block, as well as small novelty stores selling jewelry and decorations. I remember the first time I walked through Chinatown alone. I was nervous, because I did not understand Chinese. I didn't know how to request certain types of food from the restaurants, because many of them had signs that were not in English, and the workers did not speak

English either. Despite that, I enjoyed how different this community is from my own. I still admire it to this day. The difference now is I have no problem shopping in Chinatown. I am more familiar with the restaurants and not afraid to order what I want, even if it is in broken Cantonese. I'm still learning the language. The walk was relaxing and the mood felt quieter than usual. Many businesses are no more, and it's not as crowded as it used to be. It feels different now. I miss it from before, because it made me feel like I was in China even though I have never been there. I will always love Chinatown, because it is where my teaching career began. It is like my second home.

I signed up as a volunteer ESL teacher at a senior citizen center in Chinatown. I enjoy talking with the seniors. They are very kind and welcoming. I admire their desire to learn English and practice conversation. The center has other programs such as arts and crafts, calligraphy, jewelry making, and Mandarin classes. Being there, I have a chance to practice my Cantonese. "Gnaw ho jung yee gong Guang dong wah" which translates to, "I really like to speak Cantonese." I think the seniors like it when I can speak to them in Cantonese since it is their primary language. The ESL class focuses more on vocabulary and conversation. It's a very laid-back approach as opposed to a classroom setting. I like it, because it is different from what I am used to, and I really like watching the seniors interact with each other.

I am a volunteer with the American Red Cross of Greater New York. I am a volunteer client caseworker. I attended training in client casework on December 28, 2012 in disaster preparedness. After training, I worked in their call center where I helped refer clients affected by hurricane Sandy with needed resources. I met several volunteers. Seeing them in their Red Cross uniforms, and hearing their stories of deploying to different states to assist in disaster relief is admirable. I appreciate the opportunity and look forward to helping out more. I told one of the volunteers that he would see me again. When he saw me again, I said, "I'm a woman of my word aren't I?" He said, "Yes you are, and with that smile of yours and positivity you're going to make a difference here." I blushed.

Return to Rockaway and the Fractured Elbow

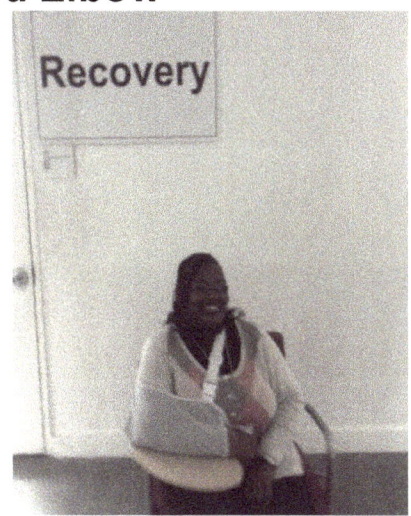

Thursday, January 17, 2013

As promised, I returned to Far Rockaway, Queens to participate in post-Sandy relief. I volunteered with New York Cares to assist at a distribution center. This distribution center serves food, and gives clothing and supplies to residents affected by hurricane Sandy. I sorted and folded clothes to prepare for the afternoon crowd. Before I could get started, I asked for directions to the ladies' room. In the midst of me saying "Thank you," I tripped over a crate and fell, my face slamming onto the hard tiled floor. I could feel my head pounding and my arm throbbing underneath my body. People rushed around me saying, "Are you okay?" When I said, "No, this really hurts," someone yelled, "Get the nurse!" I was scared. I could see my now broken glasses across the room. After the nurse examined and cleaned an open wound on my face, she helped me up. I went to an on-site clinic. I remember saying to everyone, "I'm so sorry. I am here to help ya'll out and you're helping me up!" I giggled as the nurse smiled saying, "It's okay, we want to make sure you're okay."

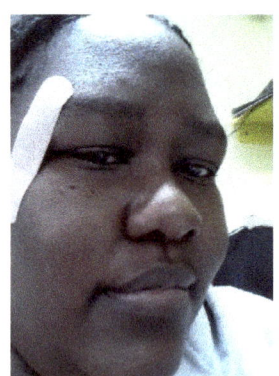

While receiving an ice packet for my swollen face, I felt woozy and achy. I had not eaten anything, which

upset the nurse. "You have to take care of yourself," she said while checking my sugar. It was low. One of the volunteers gave me a plate of food. The friend, who lost everything to Sandy, stopped by the center. It has been a year since we saw each other, yet I did not want her to see me in that condition. After a few hugs and recapping what happened, she stayed with me for the remainder of the day. She thanked me for helping out. I was just glad to see she was okay. The following week, I found out I had fractured my elbow. I'm glad it is not broken. I am thankful for the team leader from New York Cares, the volunteers, and everyone at the recreation center for their assistance and kindness. I will be back again to finish what I started.

Friday, January 25, 2013
New Writer for New York Writers Coalition

I had recently applied to be a writer for the NY Writers Coalition's blog, The Narrator. I completed an application, submitted writing samples, and had a phone interview. I wrote a practice post about mental illness versus gun control. I was nervous writing such a post since it is a broad subject, and a sensitive topic. The editors liked my article, and published it on their blog. I now write for them. I feel proud. One of my New Year's goals is accomplished, yay!

Thursday, January 31, 2013
Returning to Client Casework

After being home for a week, it felt good to return to volunteering as a client caseworker. The staff was very nice, many showing concern about my injury. One of the security officers said, "Well at least you got hurt in the process of helping others." I couldn't agree more. I was busy managing the intake process, answering phone calls, inputting clients' information into a database, scanning documents, and answering clients' questions. I volunteer in the client services department for local disasters such as house fires. It is sad to hear stories about people who are coping with devastating losses. I can't imagine how they must feel. I never experienced anything like that. I still have a lot to learn about casework, but so far, I like it. It is a great way to gain experience in a field I greatly respect, social work.

Before finishing the day, I ran into another volunteer I worked with in the call center last month. He asked what happened to me and when I told him, he joked saying I should take a picture. We were standing by a wall with a sign saying "RECOVERY." He insisted for me to look mad or sad, but when I did (which is hard for me, because I always end up laughing) he laughed out loud falling on the floor! I am not exaggerating. Between our laughter, volunteers passing by could not help but chuckle. I haven't laughed like that in a while. It felt great. The picture came out great too.

Reflecting

Sometimes, I like to take time away from social media or the laptop. I like to take a break from that and visit the waterfront to reflect. Reflecting helps put things in perspective over what is happening now. It also allows me to think about what I am doing, and where I would like to be. I go to the waterfront, because it makes me happy to watch the water's current. It is my peaceful time with self. It is my special place.

Friday, February 1, 2013
Friday Reflection

The sun is always near. It has been an interesting two weeks. I stepped away from social media, spent a lot of time by the waterfront despite the cold temps, and daydreamed. That has been my mood lately. I have been allowing my thoughts to roam free, and not focus on anything. I'm very ambitious and at times over do things. Sometimes I work too hard and don't enjoy just doing nothing. I like to daydream. It allows me to imagine, and takes me away from reality for a while. One thing I did learn from this experience is the need to take care of myself. I do not do that often, and seems like when I don't I fall. Falling the way I did two weeks ago was scary. I could hear my face hit the hard tiled floor. I felt the throbbing sensation run through my body. I still have bruises on my ankles as a result. I don't like falling and must do better in trying to avoid that from happening again. As with any new month, changes will occur. I feel a change is right around the corner for me. I will stand tall when it comes.

Thursday, February 7, 2013
Let Go, Let God. Why I Struggle to Lose Control

It is no secret that I have had my share of ups and downs in the past few months. Some of those things I cannot explain. I don't understand it myself. However, I do know how I like to feel. I know what I want to do. The only thing I have not practiced enough yet is to let go and let God. When someone says, "Let go, let God," what does that mean? For starters, it means to let go of anything or anyone that is causing discomfort in your life. The "let God" part can be interpreted in different ways. For me, it means to let God take control, giving all your worries, concerns, things you may not understand to Him. That is a struggle for me. I like to be in control of what I do. I am a proud person, I think independently, and do not always ask for help. I like to take care of things on my own. The problem with this, although positive, is the stubborn behavior that follows those traits. When you always want to be in charge, it is difficult to surrender when you have lost that control. With my recent fall, I realized that always wanting to be in control has gotten the best of me. It has affected my health as a result. My problem is trying to do everything. I have many interests and I'm very inquisitive. I like to challenge myself in doing all the things I want (career wise), be successful at them all, and still have time to help others (volunteerism, friendships). I love it and strive to continue at it. Sadly, I tend to learn the hard way that I cannot do that, because with gain there is loss. I lose in not enjoying myself in recreational things. I lose by not taking care of my needs. I lose by not making myself the focus. What's the solution? Let God.

For the first time in a very long time, I am not worrying about anything. I am not concerned about rules, the he says and she says, none of that. I don't even think about it. I still care and still strive for what I want. That will never change. However, I do not want to run the rat race. I just want to daydream. I want to meditate. I want to sing even though I cannot, and dance under the sun. I want to stare at the water, and watch the boats pass by at the waterfront. I want to take pictures. I want to drink chai latte and go to cafes just to smell coffee brewing. I want to walk through neighborhoods I haven't seen, and return to those I admire. I want to write on my notepad at an outside seating area, and watch people interact with each other. I want to download every song I love, and create playlists that I will listen to forever. I want to visit an art store, buy some paint and create a masterpiece, my masterpiece. I want to continue making things out of lanyard and re-learn how to sew. I want to smile and laugh for no reason. I want to be around people who are free-spirited and don't mind being silly. I want to have fun. What's the solution? Let go.

To let go and let God is a learning process. I am learning as I continue in my journey one day at a time.

Valentine's Day and Being Single

I usually don't like Valentine's Day. Maybe it's because I never fully celebrated the holiday. I celebrate love. As a single woman, I have gotten used to being alone. When I was a teenager, I would become depressed by watching all my friends receive heart-shaped balloons, roses, and chocolate candy. I would feel jealous watching them arm and arm with their mates. I never had a boyfriend in high school. Once, I had a friend surprise me with a rose and asked to be his Valentine. I accepted. Although we were friends, I appreciated him for thinking of me. When I became an adult, I attempted celebrating V-day with past boyfriends, which never really mattered to them. Valentine's Day no longer makes me feel sad or less loved. In fact, I feel good knowing that I love others and myself. On a day when we are taught or even pressured to have a mate, I am okay not having one. I guess I have matured over the years.

Love is beautiful; it is a powerful emotion that should be celebrated every day. I am not knocking Valentine's Day or its meaning. I think we should not wait for one day out of the year to express love. Being single is not always easy, but it's a journey to understand me more. I may not have the romantic kind of love, but I'm willing to wait for it. Waiting for love is a process. It is not an easy thing to do and takes effort. I believe that loving self must come first in order to love others. Once that happens, the cycle of love begins, and people will gravitate to that love. I rather wait for something good to come than snatch anything that comes my way. I've asked guys out, I've chased, I've loved, and yet I am still alone. I am not upset about that, because they were lessons learned. It is not worth losing my self-respect to throw myself at men. I rather a man approach me. I look forward to the day when that happens.

Post-Hurricane Sandy: Volunteerism

Saturday, March 2, 2013
Moving Moments

I had the opportunity to shadow a caseworker. I have been learning a lot volunteering at the Red Cross, and I am enjoying the process. It is not easy, but it's a great eye opener to learn what people are going through. It definitely tests one's strength. I have already had moments where I wanted to cry. The stories I hear are moving. I wish I could do more to help the clients. I guess I am always going to feel that way. The professional aspect of it is challenging too. I have been taking webinars to advance my skills in client casework. I created a binder of all my notes, handouts and training materials. My manager and caseworkers were happy and surprised I went through all the trouble. When I am serious about something, there are no limits to pursuing my goals. In the hallway near the office, I saw a table with a bowl of candy inside. Next to the bowl was a note of thanks to all the volunteers. Seeing that made my day. Although I have only been with the Red Cross since early January, I feel a part of the team. I am happy to work as a client caseworker and manage the intake process, but I am more proud just to be a volunteer.

Returning to Far Rockaway

In an effort to say "thank you" to everyone who helped me when I fell in January, I returned to the distribution center to volunteer. I, along with other New York Cares volunteers, prepared and packaged meals to give to residents. We took turns handing out hot meals, bags of canned food, and water to incoming residents to the center. I was in charge of giving out bottles of water. Majority of the people who came wanted water. I learned from the team leader that the water quality was not good in the area due to sewage leaks. I also learned that distribution efforts might stop due to a lack of food donations. There was a decrease in volunteers, and the center was not staying open 7 days a week as before. That was disheartening to hear. As I gave out the bags of bottled water, many smiled saying thank you. What made me feel sad was majority of the people coming in were elders and children. A little boy, who could have been 4 years old, wanted to help his mommy by attempting to take the bag of water. Instead, I gave him a box of macaroni. He gave me a high five and smiled holding the box. Another resident was an elderly woman who struggled to hold the bag of water. I put it in the cart for her. She thanked me and said, "You're alright." Hurricane Sandy has affected so many communities like this one in Far Rockaway but sadly, these residents have been struggling before Sandy hit. It is going to take time for people to recover from this event. Personally, I want to continue helping. We cannot forget our neighbors.

Happy 32nd Year of Life

Monday, April 22, 2013

"I thank you Lord for allowing me to be here."

I woke up a little after 9am. As I stretched my arms out, the sunlight was beaming through my empty room. I rubbed my eyes so I can see the light. I smiled and sat up to say my prayers. Last week was a hard week of cleaning, and putting things in storage after having a bed bug outbreak in my apartment. My back and hip were sore. After prayer, I noticed my phone was buzzing, and it was Facebook and Twitter messages. My smile grew bigger by the amount of birthday wishes I was receiving, especially on Facebook. I felt honored. My mom walked in the room and said, "Happy birthday Professor," giving me a hug. I thanked her as she said, "Any comments?" I said yes and showed her my Facebook profile page. She was surprised too.

While drinking tea and eating a bagel, I admired our empty space. We worked hard getting the apartment exterminated, and throwing away unnecessary stuff. It's clean and more spacious. I like it. Mom asked me, "How do you feel?" I replied, "I feel happy, because I'm just glad to see another year." Mom sipped her coffee and then asks, "What are your plans for today?" "Nothing," I smiled, "I didn't make any plans and glad I didn't. Since my birthday fell on a Monday, it is hard to plan something when it's a workday. As for today, I am just going with the flow." We sat and talked for an hour. She received a call, and I went back on social media to see the endless happy birthday messages. I responded to them all.

"I'm used to giving my all to people, so when it happens to me I don't know how to be"

On Sunday, I was overwhelmed with joy when I received a beautiful fruit arrangement from my friends from the Mocker Trail Team group on Facebook. That was truly unexpected. I felt honored. I held back tears, because I was just expressing to my mom that at times I don't feel important. That is when the doorbell rang. God is good. I thank them all for thinking of me. Two Fridays ago, I went out with some Trail Team members and friends for dinner. We were so busy talking and laughing that we almost did not order anything. As I looked at the menu, I heard, "Hello...happy happy." When I looked up, I saw my dear friend smiling at me. I said in a soft voice, "Mocker." I quietly laugh at myself, because the way I said his name (and probably the way I looked), is something you would see in a soap opera. I can be so dramatic when I am around him! I thanked him for coming and told him he is my gift. He smiled at me, and that made my night. I really had a nice time with everyone. I appreciate them for celebrating my pre-birthday with me.

Shortly after I got dressed to go to the store, I received another fruit arrangement and flowers from my dad. I felt great. Even at 32, I still love receiving balloons. I will always love receiving flowers. They make me smile. The fruit is delicious. I went out to the store, and bought some Chinese takeout and a slice of cake from my friend's store. I came back in time to watch PIX11 news and the "5@5" with Tamsen Fadal and Mocker. For fun, I had Mom take a picture of me in front of the TV. I tweeted them with the caption, "Celebrating my #bday32 with my friends." I can't help it, I love watching PIX11 news.

"Thank you for making my special day more special"

After Mom and I had dinner, Dad stopped by. I gave him a big hug and thanked him for the surprises. "Thank you both for giving me life and for just being here. That means more to me than anything else," I said to them as I tried not to cry. I'm such a water bag! My dad smiled and said, "Thank you for being who you are." My brother later came in and wished me a happy day. I think he was happy to see me happy. He knows how I have been feeling lately. He is not the expressive type, but his actions let me know how he feels. Around 9pm, I made a video thanking everyone for making my special day more special. I shared it on Facebook.

Life after Hurricane Sandy Continues

Monday, May 6, 2013
South Street Seaport

I have wanted to see the Seaport since hurricane Sandy hit us six months ago. I still cannot believe it has been six months already. Once I got off at the newly renovated Fulton Street station and saw the new World Trade Center, I could feel a difference. As I approached the Seaport, there were barricades and construction equipment everywhere. As I walked, closer to the now gated up hub for shops and restaurants, more stores had huge locks and boards with signs saying "Due to Hurricane Sandy…" It felt like a ghost town. Even the cobblestone did not feel the same. Few people were out, mostly tourists taking pictures. Fulton Market has gates around it. The restaurants that used to generate many people were gone. I took pictures but the more I snapped, the worst I felt. The mall was empty. Some people sat on the benches talking with others while some pointed at stores with hardly anyone in them. The booths that sold jewelry and other novelties were closed. One booth was open with a man standing by looking at his cell phone. Each floor was like this; even the food court on the top floor was empty. I walked through it observing the empty chairs and tables. Bars and small eateries were also closed.

I went outside where I usually go to reflect. The wood had splits in it, and the chairs and benches looked weathered. I stood by the railing and looked across at Brooklyn Bridge Park. How tiny it looked from the Seaport. The weather was nice, sunny with a cool breeze. I eventually sat at one of those reclined seats, turned on my music, and began to reflect. Looking at the Brooklyn Bridge, I tried to imagine how it must have looked when Sandy hit. I still cannot imagine how high the water rose leaving the Seaport practically under water. I also reflected on the many experiences I had at the Seaport. I remembered the times I reflected, went on dates, ate at the local restaurants, bought seashells, and took pictures. I always remembered how busy it was especially during the summer season. To see it empty was overwhelming but understandable. When I looked again, I was the only one sitting there. It was 5pm. I knew it was time for me to leave.

Before I left, I went to my favorite candy store. I love their "jelly bellies" (jellybeans) and caramels. I grew up liking caramels from my grandmother who loved eating them. The owner and I were the only ones in the store. I started talking to him asking about the effects of hurricane Sandy. He shared with me that stores like his will close by the end of the year. Plans to revamp the Seaport were in the works. He told me that they are looking for retail spaces and places to relocate. When I asked how business been since Sandy, he said, "Not good." As I left, I felt sad. I can't imagine the Seaport without the small businesses. The small businesses is what make the Seaport what it is. I walked towards the gate by Fulton Market and looked through it. "What will become of the Seaport in the near future?" I thought to myself. I don't think the

Seaport will ever be the same again thanks to Sandy, and that is not a good thing.

Wednesday, May 15, 2013
Field Client Casework

I participated in field client casework. Since volunteering as a client caseworker, I heard about field casework, and the hands-on experiences volunteers face while in the field. This was a first for me since I have only experienced in-office casework. It was also the first time working with volunteers at the Emergency Communications Center (ECC). The ECC is where responders dispatch to local disasters. Responders from the ECC conduct damage assessment and field casework. I, along with two other volunteers traveled within the boroughs to assist clients affected by hurricane Sandy. Although it has been six months since hurricane Sandy, people are still without a home. They struggle every day to take care of themselves and their families. Most of these

clients had children, which makes it even more heartbreaking. I reflected on the evening and felt accomplished. I prayed for the clients we met, and for so many who are still struggling. I am grateful I had this experience.

Friday, May 17, 2013
New York Cares Team Leader: Returning to Far Rockaway

I volunteered with New York Cares again, but this time as a team leader. I led a group of volunteers to the distribution center in Far Rockaway, Queens. I never led a group of volunteers before and was nervous at first. Once my team arrived, I didn't feel nervous anymore. They were personable and have volunteered at this distribution center previously. "And to think I had my team leader speech all prepared!" I said to them as we laughed. Once the driver came, we got in the van and headed out. There was a lot of traffic, and it took us about an hour to get to the center. We met one of the volunteers who have been

volunteering at the center since hurricane Sandy arrived. I was reacquainted with the staff. I didn't see the nurse who helped me when I fell in January. I wanted to thank her in person. We distributed sandwiches and dried goods. The center has pulled back on its operations due to less donations and fewer volunteers. I hope these efforts will continue, because many residents still need help. We stayed for three hours. I thanked my group for a job well done. They thanked me for being their team leader.

The Hip

My hip has a mind on its own. Since the surgery in 2012, I have been walking well, and have not had to use the cane much. I went to physical therapy for a short time. I decided to stop; because once I felt comfortable to walk without the cane, I felt physical therapy was no longer necessary. My ego got the best of me. Although I was walking and feeling everything was "fine," I didn't pay attention to the small signs of discomfort. My hip doctor told me that achiness is part of the healing process, and that it may occur often. I did not mind, I just kept walking. When I fell while volunteering in Far Rockaway, I did not know I might have aggravated the hip. Yet, I ignored the signs. In May, the discomfort went from an ache to actual pain. One morning I woke up and could not move my left leg. The hip cramped in such a way that it was almost impossible to move. This happened before and it scared me. I laid on my bed and began to pray. I wondered if history was repeating itself. I felt sad for a moment, and quickly put my thoughts elsewhere. I stayed home for a couple of days, took medicine, and prayed for the hip pain to go away. The pain eventually stopped. I took a walk without; you guessed it the cane. Once again, my ego would not allow me to deal with reality.

Having this hip condition is more than a physical condition it is an emotional rollercoaster. I never thought I would be living with constant pain, or relying on a cane to walk. My self-confidence was dwindling by the minute. Although I never considered myself a beauty, I do take pride in how I look. Walking with a cane made me feel inadequate and unattractive. My first thought was, how would any man find me attractive with this thing? I had this misconception that walking with a cane means old age, laziness, or that something was wrong. Those misconceptions made this process difficult to cope. That would probably explain why I rushed to walking without the cane. I also got tired of the looks and sneers from people.

When I walk with the cane, it reminds me of how I felt before losing my job. I did not like the constant questions and doubts about my condition. I hated that it hindered me from teaching. I feel that played a part in the layoff. I felt bad, but after losing a job I loved, I felt broken. That brokenness keeps me feeling insecure. Not able to do simple activities, going to many doctor's appointments and taking pain medications, all contributed to this brokenness. The worst part is having people around me claiming they are supportive yet their actions shows otherwise. I no longer felt apart of anything, and I blamed the hip for it. I was hurt having some "friends," say they care yet turned their back when I needed them most. I lost trust and still have a hard time trusting people who say they care about me. Since the surgery, I have not had much luck finding ESL teaching positions. I applied with the thought, "Can I teach with a bad hip?"

I didn't want a repeat of my last experience. Despite my efforts, I began feeling discouraged. There were no calls, interviews, or responses. I felt like my resume was getting lost in the virtual world. I tried to keep myself busy, yet I felt depressed.

Tuesday, June 11, 2013
The Cane Returns

I began using my cane again. Surprisingly, walking with it didn't bother me as much as I thought. In fact, I feel relieved to have something to help keep my balance. I am not looking forward to the stigma that comes with it, or the questions of "what happened to you," or "you're walking with it again?" My thoughts to that is as long as I can walk, that is all that matters. I will see my hip specialist if this continues. I just pray it is nothing serious.

Monday, July 15, 2013
An Update on the Walking Dilemma

I went to see my hip specialist at the hospital. I wanted to let him know about the increasing pain I've been having since late May. I also mentioned the fall I had in January. I told him, I don't know if that plays apart in my current situation but I am glad it is noted. As he examined me, he knew the level of pain by the difficulty I had lifting my left leg. Once he pressed into my left hip, I yelled "Ouch!" My doctor said, "Hmm, this isn't good, too much pain. Let's get you an X-ray." I got the X-ray but my doctor wasn't available to look at it. I had a large envelope of my X-ray and the CD that accompanied it. His assistant scheduled me for a MRI the following Friday.

When I left the doctor's office, I headed to the subway. When I got on the train, a woman was nice enough to offer me her seat. Once I sat down trying to maneuver my large envelope, I felt worried. The music in my ears wasn't helping. No song could take away the thoughts roaming through my head. I am not a fan of MRIs. The closed in capsule feels weird, and the loud noises from the test makes me feel uncomfortable. This would be the fourth MRI I had in a three year period. The first one was in 2010 and the other two were in 2011. I should be used to it. I had hoped that the last one would have been it. I guess I was wrong. The biggest worry I have is hearing my doctor say I need another surgery. I don't want that, because it is painful and the recovery time is three months. When the train pulled into the Canal Street station, I noticed the woman, who gave me her seat, looking at me intently. She was sitting across from me. She looked at me with concern. Maybe it was my face expression. I do not do well in hiding my emotions, especially on my face. As I looked away, I looked at my cane. "Is this my fate?" I said to myself.

My stop arrived and I got off to transfer to another train. I tried to stop thinking about this walking dilemma.

Tuesday, August 6, 2013
My Candid Truth

What do you do when you have done all you could? Cry? Get angry? Sit in silence? My body is having its own party, which I did not know about. It is a real pain in the ass! There are many theories as to why I am having so much pain, especially in my hip and lower parts of my body. I could blame it on the fall I had in January where I fractured my elbow. I could blame it on weight or lack of exercise. I will take responsibility for that one. Otherwise, I am not sure. The worst part of this experience is not being able to sit or stand for a long period (or in my case short period) of time. I have taken the "don't take things for granted" saying more seriously.

The other worst part of this experience is what it does to you both mentally and emotionally. The constant "what if" thoughts can drive one crazy; wondering if this condition will worsen over time. The feeling of disappointment saturates the soul. It makes you feel like you are not moving forward the way you want. In three years, I have been at more doctors' offices than I can count. I've endured bad attitudes, bad service, little answers, countless exams, and surgically tampered with. Not to mention feeling the same way I did before this fiasco happened. This has also been a lonely experience. It's sad and I don't like saying this, but when one gets sick, people tend to stay away. This is based on my own experience. In the past, this bothered me. Now, I don't care. I have become accustomed to being alone. I appreciate those who check in on me, or send encouraging messages. It means a lot.

My Book Project

Sunday, August 11, 2013

The time has come that I write a book. I am excited by this new project, because it has been a dream of mine to have something published. I have already began the process of writing things I may or may not put into my book. I did some revisions and organizing. Yet, I am left with the question, what kind of book am I writing? I think this is the hardest part of the book writing process. I have all these ideas and thoughts I want to share with the world. Except there is one concern, will people be interested in what I have to say? What can I write about that will be of interest to the reader. Gosh, I sound like a salesperson! I have been researching on the book writing business, and found that writers must be concerned in what people want to read. The target audience is very important. The subject matter is important, as well as presentation.

Okay, I have my work cut out for me.

I have been writing for years. I have journals with pages of written stuff. My stuff. I am not sure if that stuff is going to make someone pick up my book and buy it. I should note that I am not writing a book to make money. This is for personal fulfillment. It would feel great to say that I am a published author. Oh, the thought of that makes me happy. However, I still want to give it my best just in case my book actually sells. I have my homework to do. I am just excited to be tackling something I've put off for years because of fear. I still have some fears of rejection. Yet, I am ready to have my thoughts read.

Saturday, August 24, 2013
Feeling Out of Place: My Endless Circumstance

The past few days have been reflective. I have been thinking a lot about the next steps in what I am doing now, and what I want to do by the end of this year. I like thinking ahead, but try not to plan. I rather live for the moment. Lately, my moments have been quiet. Some moments are filled with sadness and loneliness. I find myself alone most of the time. Part of this is a choice and part of it is not. The sadness comes from environment, and my current health problem. I am always in pain. I do not like where I live.

I wish I lived in nature, and be around people who are friendlier and less negative.

Sometimes, I feel so out of place. I don't follow trends, I'm not skinny, and I don't have rude characteristics. I like to smell good and dress comfortable. I like to be neat. I care about working in the helping profession. I care about people. I'm not a drinker and not into the bar scene. I don't mind having a drink or two, but not interested in getting drunk or falling off a barstool. I am clueless about dating, simply because I have not had many experiences. I feel different from most. I think I either intimidate men (at least those I came across), or do not fit the societal image…whatever that is!

I feel I am a different kind of pretty, the kind that would take a special person to see. The loneliness is from disappointment I have with some people in my life. When I let my guard down and open my heart, it is taken for granted. It seems the more I do for others, the more expectations. The more expectations, the less appreciation, and the less appreciation, the more I am dismissed. I am tired of being dismissed. I don't express myself to others as much as I used to, because of this reoccurrence. I pray instead. I sit by the waterfront to reflect. I have a notebook in hand and music in my ears. Sometimes, I write, sometimes I don't. Often times, I just sit there. I pray a lot which helps, because I know my words will not go in vain. God always listens. My hope is for change to occur soon. I believe it will, and it is something I strive for all the time. Someday I will be able to walk away from this circumstance, and regain happiness. For now, I have work to do.

Sunday, September 1, 2013

I have been home for two days unable to move around or stand up straight. It is as if the body decided to go on strike at my expense. It is one of the most agonizing experiences for me, since I do not like being still for too long. Living with constant pain is hard. It is as simple as that. Stubbornly, I still try to keep my mind occupied. I have been reading everything from articles on mental health, to stories about finding love. I read the news, trends in publishing, writing, anything that sparks my interest. When I am not reading, I watch cooking shows. For someone who doesn't cook often, I enjoy watching these shows. The food looks delicious and who knows, I may try a new recipe. I return to the doctor this month for a follow up. I had a hip injection and several tests. The tests' results were good. However, the hip injection didn't help much. I hope to get answers to solving this problem. I do not want to live with pain for much longer.

The Seaport Goodbye

Thursday, September 5, 2013
A Final Walk to the South Street Seaport

I went for a walk with my mom. I enjoy spending time with her, because we get to share ideas and have fun. We always have fun in doing the simplest of things like having coffee at a cafe. I can talk to mom about anything, which is great since she is the only person I truly trust. I appreciate her more than she knows. We took a walk to the South Street Seaport. I am glad we did since we learned that it would closed this Monday. Plans for redevelopment are underway, and it will not be open until 2015. A nice man spoke to us as we passed by his jewelry and wallet table. He is from Turkey and his personality made me smile. He said it is hard to meet nice people in New York City.

"Everybody so rude, hard to be nice," he said. I couldn't agree more. I've lived here all my life and I

don't like the rude behaviors people show here. New York City is great for business and its endless resources, but it could be more welcoming in the people department. I am used to manners and pleasantry. Most people I meet think I am from the south, because of my mannerisms. My family is from the south so it makes sense.

We visited a candy store, which was practically empty. The woman there was super nice. I could feel her energy the moment we entered the store. She is a musician, and she played her album for us. Her voice is beautiful. One song really hit home, because it talked about finding happiness. She sang along and my tears flowed. That never happened to me. I usually don't cry in front of people so suddenly. I was surprised, but her music moved me to tears. I explained to her how difficult things have been for me lately, and seeing my favorite place closing makes me sad. She said that what we say in the universe would come to fruition. If one believes and speaks about what they want, it will come true. I told her I needed to hear that. I thanked her for showing empathy. We got some candy, which she offered to us free. Although we offered to pay for it, she insisted we take it. I gave her my card. I look forward to us keeping in touch.

Seeing so many stores still closed since Hurricane Sandy is disheartening. However, knowing the Seaport will close completely makes me feel worse. This is one of my favorite places to visit, especially when I need to reflect. Before going to the waterfront in Brooklyn, the South Street Seaport was my favorite destination. Although it will reopen in 2015, it will not be the same. I love the vendors and small businesses. I am not into high-end retail stores. I *prefer simplicity. I am happy mom and I had a chance to sit by the waterfront, take pictures, and admire the landscape. I will miss the original South Street Seaport.*

A Second Opinion

The hip has been hurting more than usual. It felt the way it did in 2011 when I found out I needed surgery. Instead, I wanted to get a second opinion. I made this decision, because I was afraid of what my doctor would say. I figured that if I see another doctor, he would put my fears to rest. Despite the fact that every step I take feels like someone is kicking me in the legs, I wanted to believe this was all in my head and just a temporary problem. I called several hip specialists and found one at a nearby hospital. I made an appointment. Afterwards, I felt bad. I didn't think I would be dealing with this again. I did not want history to repeat itself.

Sunday, October 6, 2013
Hope and Motivation

"You need to be the voice for so many of us who are in need. This is your calling it is embedded in you. Follow your dream."—Dad

My dad visited mom and I yesterday. I was quiet since I was not feeling my best. I am always happy to see my dad, but felt bad I didn't offer much conversation. As mom and dad talked, I sat on the couch listening when the topic of motivation came up. I asked dad how one stays motivated when things aren't going right. He simply said, "You take it one day at a time.

146

*You don't focus on what's bothering you, but stay
occupied." I brought up how I have been feeling
regarding a possible second hip surgery, being out of
work, graduate school, boredom, and me. I admit it is
a lot to say in one breath, and even harder to analyze
it all. For a moment, dad nodded his head and didn't
say anything. Mom said that I worry too much and
need to let things take its course. Dad took a deep
breath and said, "Well…" I knew he was going to
saying something that will either make me feel
confident or leave me wondering for answers.*

*"You need to go for your dream. I see it—you are
meant to help people and be their voice. You need to
be the voice for so many of us who are in need. You
need to be their representative and be the change
that is so desperately needed. It is embedded in you.
Follow your dream. Don't let this setback stop you
from moving forward." I smiled. He continued by
commending me for taking steps to feel better.
However, he wonders if surgery is necessary. He
does not want me to have another one.*

Tuesday, October 8, 2013
Getting a Second Opinion about My Hip

*I went to see the orthopedic doctor for a second
opinion. I had an X-ray done and evaluation on my
condition. The X-ray showed more than I anticipated.
Sadly, it is not just a labral tear in the hip, which was
the cause for having the first surgery. This time, it is
my hipbone. I have Degenerative Arthritis of the Hip.
It has gotten worse since my first MRI and there is no
cure for it. The bone is not in place and as a result
causes problems in walking, sitting, and standing.
Since the bone protrudes out more than it did before*

147

the first surgery, it is likely it will worsen over time. The doctor told me that he does not specialize in hip arthroscopy. His concern is I may need hip replacement if the bone deteriorates or breaks. Surgery will help, but it will not completely stop the arthritis or the pain. I like the way he explained everything to me. I am also glad I read up on my condition prior to the appointment. I was able to understand the medical terminology the doctor said. I made an appointment with my main doctor to discuss my options, but I have a feeling he is going to push for surgery since the hip injection I had in August did not work. What a mess!

Grad School on Hold

I decided not to attend graduate school. This was a difficult decision. I still want a Master's degree, I still love social work, and I still want to help people. However, financially I cannot afford it. Health wise, I am not sure what the near future will look like for me. I am not ready to tackle such a huge responsibility. I love to learn, and will continue to do so on my own time. Recently, I discovered that with my 3 degrees, along with certifications, I could still pursue the things or careers I want. Helping people is universal so I have no doubt I will be doing this for the rest of my life. Career wise, I have many options I did not know I had. I will teach again. As for social work, I know I cannot claim the title "social worker" without a degree in it. However, I have a degree in human services, another in liberal arts, and one in English. I am going to be fine. Lastly, I will continue to volunteer, because I love helping communities in need.

A Second Hip Surgery

I went back to my hip doctor for a follow up. We had a nice conversation. He examined me and expressed concern about my level of pain. I have been exercising, I did the injections, and I am always taking painkillers, and of course had surgery. I got another X-ray, and after my doctor looked at it, he said in a low voice, "We're going to go forward with surgery and hope it will relieve the pain. It is either that or hip replacement. You're too young for that." I agree with him. I don't want hip replacement. I said, "Okay, let's get this over with so I can live again." The surgery was set for December 12.

Happy National Novel Writing Month

Monday, November 4, 2013

Happy National Novel Writing Month! I am proud that I am participating this year in trying to accomplish writing a novel of 50,000 words. The goal is to have a completed manuscript by the end of the month. This is by far not an easy task. Luckily, I have a lot of writing material, but putting it together takes work. I have a long way to go with only 6,000 words written so far. So, what am I writing about?

I am writing a book about reflection with a touch of inspiration. I want my book to be unique and not a "how to" type of read. I will not claim that if you listen to what I say that you will feel better. I am not a psychologist nor am I a wisdom-filled guru that can promise good fortune. This book tells my story with a twist. I will share how reflection has helped me get through life's trials and tribulations. I hope that it will be inspiring and heartfelt. For me, this experience is not about being competitive or a bestseller novelist. Writing a book is a personal goal. It has been so for many years. It's exciting to be my own cheerleader in making my dream a reality. All I want is to have an ISBN number attached to my book. Then I will know I am a published author.

Countdown to Surgery Yet Again

Preparing for surgery is never easy. I always try to convince myself that it is no big deal and everything will be okay. Yet, I feel nervous, scared, and sad. The first time I did not prepare for surgery well. I spent time focusing on how much it is going to hurt, and the inability to walk. I was told those emotions are normal, especially for the first time experiencing surgery. This time, I still felt nervous but more stubborn not to let it bother me. I laugh about it more, and developed an attitude that this will be the last time I will experience hip surgery. When talking about my hip, I personalize it by using the pronoun "she." I feel my body is a geologic map; it is always shifting and changing. The hip is no different; *she* has a mind on her own. Since I know that, I continue to walk one-step at a time.

The Adventures of Dara Kirstene

Friday, November 22, 2013

The past couple of weeks have been nice. I have been doing everything I can to keep my spirits up, and enjoy this fall season. I also want to do as much, and see as many people as I can before surgery next month. I feel differently this time around. Positive attitude is everything.

I've always liked to pick leaves. I used to do it a lot as a child. I like the fall, because of the leaves' changing colors. The leaves this year are unique and prettier. I grabbed some plastic bags and collected as many as I could. I plan to preserve them and possibly display them on my wall. I visited some local parks and admired the changing trees. I love nature. Walking along scattered multi-colored leaves makes me feel happy. The weather has been nice with temperatures in the 60s. I know winter will arrive soon. In many ways, I am glad my surgery is happening before winter begins. When it arrives, I will be indoors. Snow is okay, ice is my enemy. They are part of the reason why my hip is the way it is. Leaf picking is more than just admiring its colors. It reminds me of something I used to do as a child. I feel I have forgotten how to be happy once I became an adult. I miss when life was simple and easy. I cannot control my circumstances to a certain extent, but I can control how I deal with it. I reflected a lot while walking through tree lined blocks admiring the leaves on the ground. In the park, I enjoyed watching the sun reflect its light through the hanging tree limbs. Its shadow effect is pretty.

The Artist in Me

One of the things I didn't do during my first surgery is prepare for it mentally. During the recovery process, I became bored and missed being outside. This time will be different. I love art, and I used to create things in the past such as drawing pictures, painting, and doing crafts. Unfortunately, I stopped. I feel art is a great way in the healing process both physically and emotionally. This year hasn't been a good one for me. In many ways, I am glad it is coming to a close. This time, I do not want to feel sad or bored. Instead, I will turn to art. I love to recycle. I also love creating things out of used items. I have been asking friends on and offline, to donate any old, used items they no longer want. These items vary from buttons, bottle tops, beads, and cardboard. Some of my ideas include but not limited to making jewelry boxes, handmade books, or wall hangings. I feel so blessed by the overwhelming response from friends. I have been receiving packages of all kinds of things for my art project. I didn't expect such a response, but so appreciative to everyone who has contributed. I will begin this project before surgery, but not after completing my manuscript.

My Mental Process before Surgery

December 1, 2013
11 Days until Surgery

I remember when it was December 2011, and I was mentally preparing for surgery. I was so scared and cried a lot. I just wanted to get through it. January 2012 arrived and I had the procedure done. I recuperated until March when I took my first steps outside. I anticipate the same this time around. I have a better attitude about it than I did in 2011. I look forward to getting better. I feel scared even when a part of me feels I should not. I have not cried, yet. I do feel a little disappointed. I know this will be a minor setback. I am just worried about the outcome. Hip replacement is always in the back of my mind. When that happens, I focus on my future endeavors. I focus on what I will create from all the things received and collected. Music and daydreaming helps too.

November was a nice month. Thanksgiving was nice too. A simple dinner from my mom, laughter from bro, and receiving free cardboard boxes from a local store, made the day nice. Simple pleasures are priceless. I already started painting and making a mess with glitter. That is the best part. I still love browsing the internet and watching Do- It-Yourself (DIY) videos on YouTube. Graduate school crosses my mind. I get several offers from schools in my email. I miss school. It is my comfort in many ways. I promised to give myself a break from academia. I want to be creative and have fun for a while before going back to school. As for my book project, I did not reach the 50,000-word mark for National Novel Writing Month. However, I did reach 25,178 words. Reaching that amount is a milestone in itself, and I am proud. I will continue working on my book and pursue publication. I hope once I am completed healed, I will find employment. I miss working. Tomorrow is my pre-operation doctor's appointment. The countdown continues.

Wednesday, December 11, 2013
The Day before Surgery

Here we go again. The nerves are elevated, emotionally I can cry on a whim, and mentally I feel tired. With all of that said, tomorrow is my second hip arthroscopy surgery. It is outpatient surgery, meaning I can go home after the procedure. I have my crutches ready. I know God will be with me so I shouldn't feel fearful. Yet, I do.

My Second Hip Surgery: Thursday, December 12, 2013

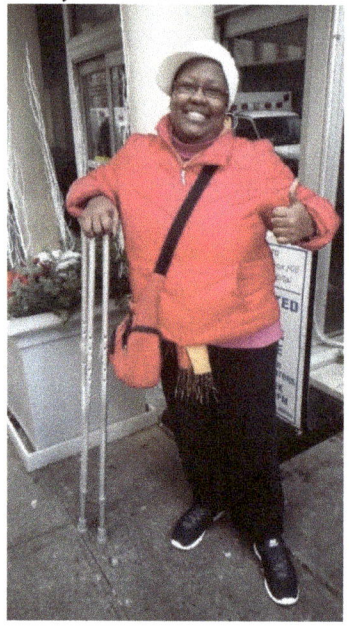

"The sun is shining bright this morning," I told mom as I observed the view from our cab ride to the hospital. I took a picture of the sun peering between the Brooklyn and Manhattan bridges. I then posted it on Facebook with a good morning message. The responses were quick and very encouraging. I felt calm. The sun was my guide.

"You're in the wrong building," the woman at the front desk of ambulatory surgery said to mom and I. "Really? This is where I had my surgery last time," I replied. The woman checked my appointment, which was at 10:30am. It was now 9:20am. She said my doctor was performing the surgery at another location. We needed to take the train to get there. We rushed to the subway and took a train to the location. As we got off, I felt like we were in a scavenger hunt! We briskly walked in the cold weather, bypassing oncoming crowds. The address that woman told us was a dentist office. I began to panic. I called my doctor's office, and the person on the phone told us that we were only a block away from the secondary location. I felt a sigh of relief.

"Welcome Ms. Fulton, we've been waiting for you," the woman at the front desk said. "Good morning, we were told to go to the main hospital only to be told to come here. But the important thing is we're here," I said. The woman was very nice. We went to a room where I needed to be registered; that is where you get that cool ID bracelet for surgery. As a nice man verified my information, my doctor walks in. I signed some forms and off I went.

"You need to take THAT off now!" a nurse yelled at me while putting my things in my assigned locker. The "that" she was referring to was a crucifix I wear around my neck. The way she said it made me emotional. She gestured in a way as if seeing it bothered her. I said okay and took it off putting it in my jacket pocket. The crabby nurse, who I overheard tell someone that she was "tired," took my blood pressure. "It's too high! This is no good!" I wanted to say, "No shit lady!" but I composed myself and looked away. I had my gown on already and was waiting to go upstairs.

When "Ms. Crabby" left, I read a few pages from a prayer book I usually carry with me. I asked God to keep me calm. I put the book in the locker. I tried to do so without Crabby seeing me. As I sat back down, another nurse approached me with mom. When they asked me how I was, I cried. The nurse put her hands on my shoulders and said, "It is okay honey." I wiped my tears saying, "I can't, I can't…my nerves." I did not realize Ms. Crabby was standing there. She rubbed my back saying, "It's gonna be alright." I didn't want her to touch me, but instead go away. Mom hugged me. The nice nurse comforted me as she escorted us upstairs via the elevator. As the doors opened, the nurse said, "This is where everyone wears pajamas, so you'll feel right at home." Everyone was in blue scrubs. I smiled. Once seated, the nurse said she wanted to take my pressure again. "Think 120 over 80" she said. I did and my pressure was lower than that. Mom and the nurse were surprised. "Good job! Now you're all set," the nurse said happily. Once the intravenous (IV) was in my arm and I met the handsome anesthesiologist (his smile was infectious), it was time to go in for surgery.

"Let me fix that for you," another nurse said fixing my gown. "We don't want you exposed," she said. As the nice nurse and mom headed to the elevator, I looked back at them saying, "Oh we can't have that, I can't be scaring people!" We all laughed as I went through the double doors. The operating room looked like a spaceship. Lights everywhere and gadgets I did not understand. I got on a narrow table that is intimidating to look at. We introduced ourselves. All I remember was mentioning how the room looked like a spaceship, and smelling the man's cologne. "Oh he smells good," I said to myself as I fell asleep.

"Ms. Fulton, how are you feeling?" a nurse asked me. Everything was a blur, and I could not see her clearly. I said in a low voice, "Hi, I'm okay. Where is my mom?" She said they were sending her up to see me. She then asked about my level of pain. It was around a six, at which the nurse gave me more medicine. "How are we doing professor?" Mom asked me while holding my hand. I didn't realize I fell back to sleep. "Hi Mommy, I'm really happy you're here." Several nurses tended to me giving me water, apple juice, and a small apple cinnamon muffin. It was so hard to eat, because I felt nauseous. Eventually, another nurse assisted mom in dressing me, and wanted to show me how to walk using the crutches. After using the restroom, the nurse showed me how to walk with the crutches. That was challenging since I kept falling asleep every few seconds. "Wake up Dara, I need you to see where you're walking," the nurse said sternly. I felt frustrated, because I couldn't help it. Whatever drug I was on to decrease the pain, it caused me to feel woozy and very drowsy. I don't like those feelings.

When we were finished, the nurse gave me a hip wheelchair, a wheelchair specifically for patients who have hip surgeries. I did not know they had such a thing. I thanked the nurse and mom for their help and patience. We took a car service home. My brother helped me upstairs to our apartment. Luckily, it wasn't as difficult to go upstairs like the first time. Yet, the pain was the same. I posted a picture mom took of me in the hospital, and posted it on Facebook and Twitter. I wanted my friends to know I was okay, and thank them for their continuous support and love. Their love and encouragement meant more to me than they may know.

Sunday, December 22, 2013
The Aftermath

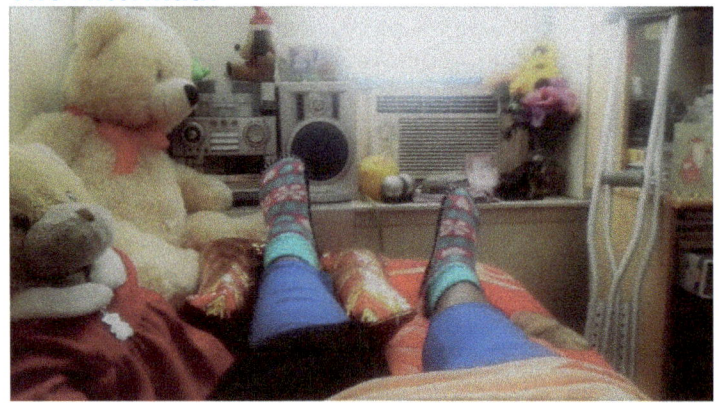

It has been a week since surgery. The first few days were challenging, since I didn't have my medicine. There was a mix up with my prescription from the doctor's office and the pharmacy. Meanwhile I took aspirin, which did not work. I finally got my prescription filled the following week. I kept my spirits up by collecting things around the house, and searched for craft ideas online. Talking with friends on social media has been a big help. I appreciate the check-in messages, and get well wishes. Before the surgery, I made some handmade Christmas cards for friends. I sent them out before the surgery. Their reactions via text messages and pictures made me smile. I received some nice cards as well.

Shortly after receiving my medicine, I became ill. I felt stressed out, because my living conditions aren't the best. Constant noise, partying all times of the night from neighbors, and bad leaks have taken a toll on my family. The leak in the bathroom was the worst. Holding an umbrella over your head while trying to pee isn't my idea of a comfortable bathroom

Post-op

I made it to my post-operation appointment. I had an ambulette pick me up from home. It was my first time being in one. I used my crutches to walk and thankfully, mom accompanied me. The driver picked up two other patients who were dropped off at different hospitals. The drive was not comfortable. It was a very bumpy ride. We must have hit every pothole along the way. Unfortunately, I forgot to wear my hip brace. I was in a lot of pain by the time we arrived to the hospital. The waiting room was packed. There were at least 20 people seated. The surgery coordinator greeted us. We waited for over an hour. I began to feel pained, and mom asked the coordinator if we could reschedule my appointment. She apologized for the wait, and said the doctor wants to see me since this was my first post-operation appointment. Ten minutes passed when I was called to the examination room. Mom came in with me. As I was getting on the exam table, the doctor came in. He asked how I was feeling. I told him about the bumpy ride as I laid back on the table. He slowly lifted my leg. It shook some but not as bad as before.

He checked the stitches and said, "They look good, we can remove them." I said, "Already?" My doctor smiled, "Yes, you heal fast, but you will need physical therapy. There was a lot of scar tissue left from the last surgery. Also, you have to lose some weight to avoid pressure on the hip." He also told me that the arthritis in my hip increased since the last surgery, and at times that will cause pain and stiffness. He also stated that if the pain becomes unbearable and further surgery is necessary, then hip replacement would be an option. He advised me to be careful in how I walk, and try not to fall. After our talk and many "thank you" comments, he left and the nurse came in. She removed the stitches, which didn't hurt as I thought. I walked out feeling relieved that I was on the road to recovery. Shortly after, I made an appointment for physical therapy.

2014

Year 2014 was an uneventful year. I applied to jobs, wrote a few blog posts on *Dara's Creative Corner*, and did a lot of reflecting. I did not write as much on the blog, because I got tired of posting the same updates of me still looking for work, my desire to teach, my stresses of where I live, blah, blah, blah. It seemed the only highlight in 2014 was turning a new age.

April and Turning 33

Tuesday, April 22, 2014
Happy 33rd Year of Life

I did a voice recording. It was a very personal voice recording, because I discussed my feelings about love. I haven't done an audio reflection in years. It felt good to release my feelings through voice, especially paying attention to changes in my tone as I talk about loving someone, wanting to be loved, and the letting go process. Staring at the horizon is where I get lost in thought. I don't hear anything except the sound of the crashing waves and seagulls squealing. I recorded that too. The thing that hit home while reflecting is how much I desire living in a natural environment. I don't want to travel to it anymore, but instead live in or near it. I recorded the sounds of the beach so I can listen to it when I am not there. I do not like my living environment. It makes me very sad, and it's something I don't talk about often. I never liked my neighborhood and not very fond of the people who I live amongst. I have been feeling this way since 1990 when my family moved to Bedford-Stuyvesant ("Bed-Stuy"), Brooklyn. That is a long time feeling the same way.

Going by the water, whether it is the waterfront or the beach is my escape from the foolishness I have to deal with at home (not with family). Sometimes, I cry just thinking about it. I think most people who know me feel I am happy all the time when in fact that is not the case. I have my sadness, and at times feel empty inside when it comes to wanting certain things. I hide it by focusing on what makes me happy: God, school, work, helping people, writing, music, and nature. Love makes me happy especially when I love others. When it is not reciprocated, that makes me sad. Working towards my goals and dreams is what keeps me going. If I did not have that, I don't know where I would be. I think a lot when I am by the water.

Grad School...again?

I applied to a different graduate school, this time majoring in human services. It was done in haste, because I wasn't sure if I was ready to go back to school. I still wanted a Master's degree. I was accepted to their online Master's program. Classes began in May and it was off to a good start. I completed three semesters, passing my classes with As. Despite how well I was doing, I began to feel depressed. I was still unemployed. I felt doubtful on this journey since money was scarce, and it affected the necessities like buying food, paying bills, and maintaining the home. I felt disheartened that I wasn't able to help my mom financially. I applied for food stamps. I received it for a few months. When I tried to recertify, I was denied. I didn't qualify for public assistance. Our housing woes continued with the noise and occasional leaks. I consulted my physical therapist about my progress with the hip. Although I was progressing well, I will continue to have hip pain and problems with balance. My balance was greatly affected since the second surgery, so much so that I lean without even knowing it. The cane has become a necessity.

Monday, June 2, 2014
Two Years Unemployed: The Difficult Journey
Continues

This has been the hardest struggle I've faced in a long time. Being financially poor and not sure how to change that has and continues to bother me. Finding work is difficult, even in my field of ESL. I feel sad that since being laid off from my last employer, I am still unemployed. This month makes 2 years I have been out of work. I put in for several positions in both ESL and other fields like administration, customer service, or emergency management. I have not had much luck in any of them. When I go on interviews for ESL positions, I am turned down. I think it is because I am either over-qualified or too passionate about teaching. I love it, what's wrong with that? I feel frustrated by some agencies who have a laid-back approach to teaching adult immigrant learners. Just because they are learning a language other than their own, that doesn't mean the approach should be less than satisfying. Sometimes the nonchalant attitude or unpreparedness of some ESL programs bothers me. I am not saying that I'm an expert, but our students deserve more than sloppy curriculums, half put together syllabi, or teachers who care more about the pay than student progress. In regards to other job positions, my experience is limited. Unfortunately, I do not feel as confident working in a new career as I do teaching English as a Second Language. Despite that, I still try my best and apply anyway.

The dreaded, *"Why am I still single?"* Stage

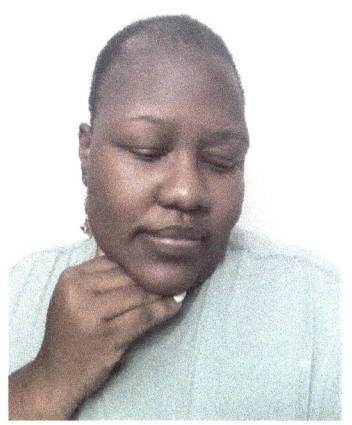

Part of my depression is the feeling of loneliness. I don't mind being alone, but hate to feel lonely. Since my last relationships, I have not dated anyone. I've had crushes and possible interests, but nothing that developed. It is disappointing when you start to grow feelings towards someone and nothing comes out of it. I guess that is part of life. I used to dislike seeing couples around me. I would feel envious. Ironically, when I visit the waterfront at Brooklyn Bridge Park all I see are couples, many of them who are taking their wedding pictures. I love weddings even though I have not been to one. I also like to see the happy facial expressions of the bride and her groom. I love wedding gowns too. I dreamed of getting married since I was a little girl. I've always said that someday I would want my wedding to be on a beach. My groom and I will be barefoot, standing along the shoreline saying our vows to each other. Someday, I hope that will come true for me.

I never had good luck with men, always meeting the wrong types. I am to blame for some of that. Not having good self-esteem tends to make one settle for less. I did that, because I did not think highly of self, and I felt I did not deserve better. I always thought I was ordinary so who was I to have preferences. The odder he was the better chance we will work out because I am odd too. I learned the hard way that was not a positive way of viewing self. I know I am not odd, just unique and creative with a big heart. I wouldn't trade that in for anyone.

Sunday, July 13, 2014
Summer Moods

This has been a reflective summer thus far. I've been quiet on this journey called life. I have not talked to too many people, nor have I posted much on social media. For the first time, my mind and heart won't allow me to express myself. I feel many things yet I cannot seem to find the words to express them. Maybe I am not supposed to. Since my mind and heart isn't allowing me to share, I pray instead. I write

also. The more I write, the better I feel releasing my feelings and thoughts. Carrying a notebook everywhere I go has become routine for me.

I went to Coney Island beach. I stood by the shoreline and reflected. I walked into the water, ankle deep without my cane. This was a gift to self, entering the water freely without any assistance. It has been a long time I could do that since my hip surgeries. I always listen to music when I am at the water reflecting. That day I listened to a cassette tape of house music I made 10+ years ago. It is special to me, because I used to listen to it a lot when I visited Rockaway beach alone. I traveled a lot by myself in the early 2000s. The music helped me not to feel nervous. Standing in the water with music in my ears felt liberating.

I have finally reached the "Why am I still single," stage. I have heard people go through it in different ways. It is the stage when (it seems) everyone around you is either married, dating, or in a relationship. I dreaded the day this stage would find me. I don't like talking about it. In my many attempts in talking to people about it, I tend to get the generic "It will happen for you someday," or having to hear how blissful their relationship is with whomever. The "one day you will be lucky to find someone like my so and so" comment is something I don't want to hear. I rather just be with my own so and so. I am always happy for those who found their love. Unfortunately, I cannot express it now especially when I am feeling so alone, and sad about being single at 33. It has been nearly 4 years since I have dated or been in a relationship. I am not convinced that those who found their love can relate to me. Why should they? I cannot relate to my single friends, because some of their ways in going about dating is not my style. So, I remain silent. Silence is not something I have always embraced. In fact, I tried to avoid it. I realized that being silent is helpful when putting things in perspective. I am nowhere near to fully understanding the transition I am in, but through patience and faith, it will come to full circle. For now, my notebook is my best friend.

That Thing Called Depression

It's September and I am writing in my journal. Writing in my journal gives me the courage to write publically on my blog. Yet, some things I only write for self. When I decided to write a book, I wanted to not only share my story, but to inspire others who may have or are going through the same things I experienced. Talking about depression is something I have avoided for years. I spoke to some counselors in my adolescence, but always masked it with a smile and "I'm okay" comment.

I was in therapy while in college. While attending Queensborough Community College (QCC), I became depressed. I got so depressed that I stopped attending classes. I eventually dropped out. Once I attended City Tech, I became more depressed. I saw a therapist for a while. It helped me become more expressive about things that made me unhappy. Eventually, I left therapy and graduated from school. Although I have had my share of hurt and pain (both physical and emotional), I dealt with it. I still struggled with loneliness and sadness. There were times where I would cry excessively, while other times I felt combative. I dealt with it. After the rape, I felt I lost control. Outwardly, I continued to smile, teach classes, and pursue a third college degree. Inwardly, I felt anger, hurt, and a desire to disappear. I never got justice for self. I allowed someone to hurt me very much, and didn't bring him up on charges. Instead, I said I forgave him and went back to a relationship that was bound for disaster. I still regret that to this day. I hate him for taking away my innocence, but I hate myself more for not doing anything *legal* about it.

I never sought counseling for the rape, or any of the things that happened to me since I left therapy in 2004. I talked with my mom and wrote down my feelings. I took a step in coming forward when PIX 11 did a segment about domestic violence. I tweeted about being a victim of sexual abuse. It was a bold move. I received some positive responses. In

September 2013, I wrote a blog post titled, "Hush! The Quiet Epidemic Called Suicide." It was about my first experience attempting suicide. It was the first time I ever wrote about it and shared it publically. September is suicide awareness month. I wanted to share my story in hopes it can help someone who is experiencing thoughts of suicide. The response I received on Facebook was unexpected. Many showed empathy, and commended me for being so honest about something that tends to go unheard. I am sad to admit this, but I have been suicidal for years. I still have thoughts of suicide. I pray to remove such thoughts and try not to feel that way. Ironically, this September those thoughts returned. On the day of a job interview, I swallowed my pride and made a phone call for an appointment. An appointment that was long overdue.

Thursday, September 11, 2014
The First Session

I'm sitting at the bar of a Starbucks, listening to some jazz-bluesy song while drowning my sorrows in hot coffee. I am having that with a slice of pumpkin loaf. I just came from my session; it is the first one, the first step to healing. I need to have a psychological evaluation. I am considered "low to mid-risk" suicidal. How sad that my life has come down to this! I thought those days have left me and instead they resurfaced. Talking about it makes me sad; I know I am better than this, or am I? So once again, I am here drowning my sorrows in coffee. I just wish I felt better. I could cry now. Opening up about my pain is hard; I have to relive those emotions, the sadness, the anger, the frustration, the loneliness, the feeling of wanting to disappear. Honestly, I don't want to die. I just want a better life, because I do believe in a tomorrow. I believe in second chances. But most of all, I love God. I cannot do that to Him, I cannot do that to my mom. I am stuck feeling what I feel, and trying to find ways dealing with that. The topic of medication came up today. I declined because I don't want something controlling my emotions. I want to have control over me.

It was difficult talking to a new stranger about my current and past problems. Although she is nice, I have my guard up. I've had my guard up for years since getting hurt. I have trust issues and do not always believe people when they say they care about me. I have to feel it for me to believe it to be true. I have loved so many people. Some I have loved more than I should. Sometimes, I wonder how they feel towards me. As the saying goes, action speaks louder than words. Sometimes the actions of some make me question their intensions. One of the hardest parts of this journey is admitting to loving men who were not good for me. I haven't met the right type of men. I love hard and when I don't receive love back, it hurts me. Then feelings of loneliness sets in. One way, I have tried to tackle this dilemma is by writing poetry. I am told that my poems have a melancholic tone. When I write about love, I feel melancholy. It isn't my intension to sound melancholy in my poetry, but my love life has always been that way. I speak what I feel in my heart.

The same goes for friendships. I had to end some friendships because they were detrimental to my well-being. Other friendships ended due to arguments, or life's circumstances. I don't have many friends, mostly associates whom I talk to sometimes. My philosophy professor once told me that I would lose friends once I progress in my life. I was surprised and asked him why he made such a statement. He said, "Because that is part of life. People will drop out of your life as you move up the ladder." That statement has resonated with me since then. I have seen that happen in my life. I've made mistakes, and that has affected some of the friendships I used to have. However, the one thing that has changed about me is I no longer tolerate being mistreated. I was once the human doormat allowing people to say and do whatever they wanted without cause. I have become more outspoken which has angered some, and they left me alone. I won't apologize for that, because everyone has the right to stand up for self. If you don't, people will take advantage. Self-worth is one of the lessons I had to learn the hard way. From past relationships to current friends, being true to self is important. Loving and accepting self is necessary to live a happy life. True friends will love you for who you are, and will not go out their way to hurt you. My professor was right.

My hope is to learn how to let go of the pain, the rejection, and the feelings of loneliness. To let go of those who have or continue to ignore or push me away, and to move forward. My hope is to live in the moment. The hardest part of dealing with depression are those lingering thoughts of suicide. It is frustrating and something I struggle with every day. I am still working out my feelings about the rape, feeling violated, and difficulty trusting others. I have fears about getting close or being intimate with a man. I have had women make jokes about me being celibate for years. I am celibate, not for religious reasons even though I feel good waiting for that special someone. I would like to fall in love and be intimate with someone again, but I would rather wait. The risk of being sexually violated again is a risk I'm not willing to take.

Everyday

Through pictures, I tell a story. Every day there is something to see, something to discover. I am discovering self. Some mornings I do not want to get up. There are times when I want the days to go by without experiencing it. Then tomorrow arrives. I wake up, say my prayers, and drink tea. I pick up the camera, the notebook, my cane, and head outside. I walk. I look up to the sky. The sun welcomes me as I take its picture. The day begins. I travel by mood. I go wherever the mind leads me. The sun is my guide. Appointments arise, interviews come and go, and I wait in many waiting rooms. If available, I stare out the window. Each view is different. My name is called, and I enter another room. The process happens. The conversation begins. With each experience, I walk away feeling melancholy. I observe new surroundings. I take a few pictures. The train stations are different. I wonder where to go next.

Date unknown, written in a notebook

I return to Starbucks, buy a latte, and sit at the bar. I pull out the notebook and begin to write. I write words that are within me. I have no control. The latte soothes me as music plays in the background. The sweet smell of coffee elevates the senses. Someone sits next to me, and looks over at what I am doing. I ignore the person. My shyness consumes me. I continue to write. Somehow, I want to hide between the lines of the notebook paper to escape reality. There I can find shelter. Shelter from the emotional turmoil, this repetitive cycle of schedules, appointments, exchange of information, discussions, applications, waiting and more waiting. The result is the same. The situation remains. I stop writing. The latte is now cold as I take the last sip. I walk outside and look up to the sky. I take a deep breath. The sun begins to set. I take a picture. I go home and reflect just to do it all over again tomorrow.

October 13, 2014
October Reflection: Visiting Rockaway

With the changing temperatures and colors of the leaves, I find myself changing as well. Life around me has been a whirlwind of good, bad, and ugly all balled up into one. Trying to explain it will be overwhelming. I do believe there is a positive to every negative, and nothing lasts forever. I visited Rockaway beach where I met my friend who lost everything to hurricane Sandy. It was nice to see her, and to catch up on some things. I saw some progression, more people moving about and stores that reopened since Sandy. However, the area I was at when I volunteered after the storm is now an empty lot up for sale. It looked different from how it did in December 2012. Walking pass that lot with her was sad. That is where her house once stood. The silence that followed us was poignant. As we walked on the beach and I stopped every minute to pick up a seashell, I could not help but feel melancholy. The beach still has its natural beauty, but one can still feel the remnants from Sandy. Although, I believe things will get better out there, I don't think it will ever be the same.

October 22, 2014
On the Road to Healing: A Mini Reflection Piece

When you are on the road to healing, you must make decisions that are not always easy to make. Often times it will require you to let go of things and people. This can be in the form of a hug, a verbal conversation, or a silent message. It isn't an easy thing to do when you care so much, when you love so much. I still struggle with this. I guess that is part of life's endless journey, the emotional aspects of each step taken, and the strength that must come from within. For me, I am guided by the sun, and like water, I flow through the process hitting every bump along the way. The greatest wish I have for those I love and care about is to be well on their journey. I hope the paths we take will lead us in the direction of our heart's desire.

"Brooklyn is my home"

On Wednesday, October 29, I walked across the
Brooklyn Bridge. I made a promise to myself that after
I recover from my second hip surgery, I would walk
across the bridge. I feel proud that not only I walked
across the bridge, but did it alone. I needed to prove
to myself that I could do it. I never walked across the
bridge alone. I love the structure of the Brooklyn
Bridge. The way the wiring connects everything
together is amazing. Depending on where you are
standing, it feels like it is coming at you like a web. I
liked seeing people take pictures. I was taking selfies.
One guy saw me and ducked his head smiling. I
giggled and said, "No worries, I am just taking a
selfie." At the middle of the bridge, I stood looking out
at the water. I saw Brooklyn Bridge Park down below.
I smiled, because that is where I usually go to reflect.

It felt nice to reflect from up above. I didn't think about much. It felt good to go with the flow. The breeze felt nice, and watching the sky change was even nicer. "Brooklyn is my home," I said to myself. "It will always be a part of me."

Transitions

I left graduate school. The news was surprising to the few people I confided in. By the last two weeks of the fourth semester, I crashed. The papers, the constant research, deadlines, and not enjoying the process all affected me emotionally. Sadly, I have not felt happy since the beginning of the second semester. I did not share that with anyone for fear of judgement. I was passing all my classes with A's, yet felt depressed. I felt embarrassed to share how miserable I was while maintaining a high grade point average. I impulsively pursued the Master's in Human Services believing that was what I wanted to study. My volunteer work during Hurricane Sandy inspired me to pursue social work/human services. I felt that was the field for me. I still like human services, but teaching is my true love. I really want to be back into my career of adult education. Since leaving school, I felt a sense of relief. I feel I can now put my focus on my creativity and find my way back to the ESL classroom. If asked whether I will return to school someday, the answer is yes.

Friday, December 26, 2014
Reflections of an Ending 2014

This holiday season has had its difficulties. With so many tragedies happening in the world and personal troubles, the Christmas season doesn't feel so merry.

Yet, this year has taught me to turn the bad into good to the best of my ability. I cannot control the world, but I can control me. It is no secret that I haven't been happy for some time, but I feel 2014 was okay. I learned a lot about myself, and embraced adulthood a little more. I cried when needed to, prayed, requested prayer from both friends and strangers, challenged self to be alone despite my struggle with loneliness, and let go of negative things and people. I made important decisions, and put me first above everything else. I put my feelings first, because I believe emotional and spiritual health is just as important as physical health. I made a promise to self to be more direct, honest, and loving to me. I also promised self not to be afraid of the unknown, and to go with the flow. I am no longer concerned with other people's opinions of me. I learned that I have to live for Dara, because I only have this one time, this one chance at this journey called life.

People

I am strengthening my friendships with people in my life while trying to establish new ones. Every year I lose or move on from old friendships. I used to be bothered by it, but now I appreciate the experience. I believe everything happens for a reason. Some people aren't meant to stay in your life. Sometimes our paths must go in different directions. I always like to move forward on good terms with people who I am no longer friends or in communication with. If that happens, I smile. If not, I still smile knowing I have no animosity towards that individual or individuals. The current friendships I have I appreciate, and hope will remain throughout New Year 2015. As for love, I am ready to explore that option as well.

Creativity

The goal for New Year 2015 is to fully explore, enhance, and embrace my creativity on all levels. I put many projects aside. There are ideas I have written down. I am ready to bring those things to the forefront. I want my book published. I want my art seen. I want to continue capturing my love for nature through the lens.

Me

I am continuing to work on myself. I hope to be here for many more years to come, and walk on more paths. I consider myself an adventurer, one who likes to travel, see, and experience new things while capturing the moment one picture, one-step at a time. I look forward to another year and an improved me.

2015

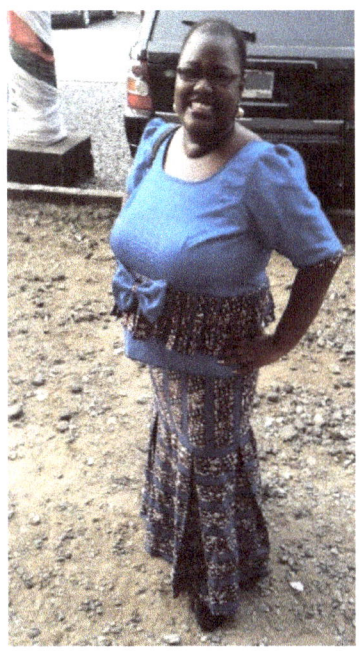

Year 2015 was a year of hopes, dreams, and possibilities for newness and success. Yet, it turned out to be a more reflective time of love and adventure.

I worked for two language schools where I taught adult learners various English classes. It was my first time teaching at a language school. It was also the first time teaching a six-hour class. Accent Reduction training was one of those classes. That was an interesting and sometimes boring course to teach. Neither the students nor I liked the textbook. To make it more interesting, we combined the material with real life scenarios and conversations. Teaching informal American speech was the students' favorite subject. It is my favorite too and the most fun to teach. At the other language school, I had a four-hour class with four students. Within a month, it decreased to two students and then to one student. It was challenging, because there was not much support in how to generate more students. The student I had wasn't happy being the only student there. Most times, we practiced English conversation. Teaching at language schools are different from teaching at non-profit organizations. Language schools are for-profit focusing on student attendance and enrollment, whereas non-profit organizations focus on community building. As in any work environment, I met some wonderful students who made my short time at those schools worthwhile.

From online love to Lagos, Nigeria

I traveled to Lagos, Nigeria in December for adventure, love, and to gain a new experience. It was the first time leaving the U.S. but ironically, I did not feel nervous. Instead, I felt excited and could not wait to put my feet on the Motherland. I remember boarding the plane at John F. Kennedy International Airport not realizing the long travel time. It would be a 9 hour and 45 minute flight to Istanbul, Turkey. Upon arrival, I would need to take a connecting flight to Nigeria. I don't think the time difference sunk in until I was on the plane. I looked at the TV screen in front near the restrooms, and I saw a map of our plane crossing the Atlantic Ocean. To know we were traveling over water with no land in sight made me feel anxious. I couldn't wait to land in Istanbul.

Once I arrived in Turkey, I felt a bit confused. Majority of the signs were in Turkish with some English translation. Finding the gate to pick up my connecting flight was difficult. Every Turkish airline worker I spoke to either didn't speak English or just said, "I'm not sure." By the grace of God, I found my gate and boarded the place with no problems. As an ESL teacher, I understand the frustration my adult students have communicating in English. I felt like those students while I was in Turkey.

I arrived in Lagos a day after I left New York. My boyfriend greeted me outside the airport. The way he hugged me is something I will never forget. He is the first man I have dated in five years. I loved the cologne he was wearing. I loved his smile. We met from a pen pal site, and I instantly fell for him. I never had an international relationship before. It felt exciting, and I knew I wanted to meet him. Although this trip happened suddenly, I didn't mind. Seeing him made it all worthwhile. I loved him. He loved me and I felt it on and offline.

I couldn't believe I was in Lagos, Nigeria. I am the first in my family to travel to Africa. My ancestry is Nigerian so this trip was both personal and reflective. I thanked God for allowing me to have this experience. I am happy my first international experience was in Nigeria. While there, I saw so many cool things, such as, women carrying items on their head, to chickens walking along the roadside. I met many wonderful and welcoming people, and ate delicious food. I loved eating native dishes like amala, joloff rice, moi moi and egusi soup. I danced to popular afro beats, and made many friends while dancing. Some even showed me how to do Nigerian dance moves. I still have to practice.

The moving part of this trip was living like a Nigerian. I remember telling my boyfriend that although I am American, I do not want any special treatment. I want to experience Nigerian culture to the fullest. I am proud that I had the chance to speak some Yoruba, and dress in native wear, which is so beautiful it makes me feel like a queen. I enjoyed greeting elders in traditional Yoruba fashion by kneeling down. I had the pleasure of greeting my boyfriend's grandmother, aunts, and his church leaders in traditional Yoruba fashion.

This trip changed my life in such a way that I want to return. It has inspired me to visit more countries in Africa and across the globe. I love meeting people of different cultures and backgrounds. I learned so much during my time in Nigeria. I returned shortly after New Year's in January 2016, but I continue to carry "Naija" (slang for Nigeria) in my heart. Although things didn't work out between my boyfriend and me, he will always have a special place in my heart. What we shared is something I never experienced with anyone and I will be forever grateful for that. I plan to write my Nigerian experience in a separate short story.

An Artsy 2016

I spent most of 2016 working on my artwork. I had an online store where I attempted to sell my recycled artwork, which included decorative glass bottles and plastic jars. Unfortunately, I didn't make any sells and eventually closed the store. I began drawing again. It started out as a doodle then to a design. I call it, "Squiggly lines, dots, and whatever else." It is a combination of lines, dots, and various shapes. It is a free form type of illustration. It relaxes me when I feel stressed.

Each drawing is based on my emotions. I had one of those designs printed on a T-shirt and a mug. I created business cards with my design on it. In June, I attended the Small Business Expo where I wore my T-shirt and passed out my business cards to potential clients. It was the first time I marketed my artwork and myself. It felt great. I drew 27 forms of "Squiggly lines, dots, and whatever else," and by August, it became copyrighted at the U.S. Copyright Office. It is an honor to have my work protected by law. I feel there is great potential to this art form, and I am excited by where it can take me. The possibilities are endless.

Present Day

January 2017
"My artistry, my voice"

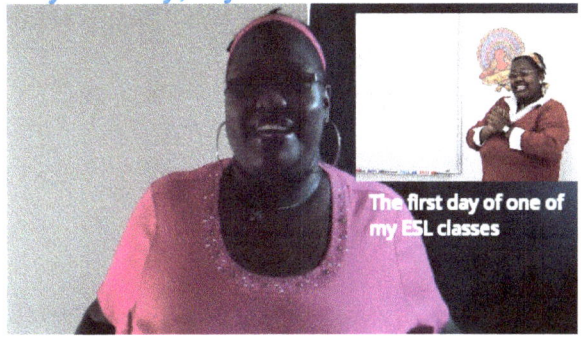

The first day of one of my ESL classes

I am a simple lady with simple ambitions and big dreams. I love "love" and enjoy expressing it. My art is who I am, different, squiggly, and colorful. Writing is my inner voice when I cannot speak. Reflection is everything. I love to teach, but enjoy learning more. Helping people is my passion. I am Me.

I am a YouTuber. I produce creative content for my YouTube channel. I started my YouTube channel in December 2010. I had 20 subscribers. Majority of my videos were life updates, motivational messages, and my time being on the news. I did not post often and my channel became obsolete. I decided to change that. By December 2016, I revamped my channel by reintroducing myself, and shared its purpose. I changed my channel's name from *DKirstene Creative TV* to my name, *Dara K. Fulton*. I am a woman of many interests and talents. I love to express myself, and help people in everything I do.

The basis of my channel is to highlight who Dara K. Fulton is, as well as, continue sharing motivational messages of hope, encouragement, and reflection. I also share entertaining videos such as Do-It-Yourself (DIY) craft tutorials, and "Get Ready With Me" (GRWM) makeup chats. Since I am not a professional crafter or makeup artist, these videos are fun to make and watch. And yes, I re-watch my videos whenever I need a laugh! By January 2017, I decided to include my love for English as a Second Language (ESL) into my videos. I started a video series and blog both called, *Motivation for the ESL teacher and ESL student.* I create videos and blog posts about teaching English as a Second Language. I also discuss ways students can learn English outside the classroom, and ways both teachers and students can stay motivated.

Since the launch of my revamped channel and new video series, my subscriber count has went from 20 to 100. For me, that is a great accomplishment in such a short amount of time. I am honored to every person who watches, likes, and comments on my videos. I appreciate everyone who subscribes to my channel. I am not concerned about being a famous YouTuber with millions of subscribers or video views. I love creating content for the public to watch. Most of all, I love sharing my passion for ESL to the world. Helping people continues to be my life's goal. I am grateful that YouTube allows me to do that.

Lastly, I started a mini motivational series called, *Coffee with Dara: offering motivation and encouragement to the world*. This started as a short video I posted on Facebook and Instagram. I received great responses and decided to keep making videos. I call these videos, *Coffee with Dara*, because I am drinking coffee while I am recording. I want my audience to feel like they are having coffee with me as I am offering some encouraging words to them. Each video has a specific topic such as, "Never give up," or "Do not compare yourself to others on social media". Although I am no longer on Facebook, I continue to post *Coffee with Dara* videos every Monday and Friday on Instagram.

I call this, "My artistry, my voice" year. It is the year I am allowing the world to see, listen, and witness my art in its many forms. Filming and editing videos is new and is now part of my art. I believe the sky is limitless. I do not know what the future holds for me. All I know is I must live for today. I am living for the moment.

This Is Not the End to My Story

My personal life still has its challenges. I still want to move somewhere else, and I am looking at teaching opportunities overseas. Stress continues to be a major factor to my physical and mental health. I am still working out my problems through prayer and counseling. I believe this is a step-by-step process, and I am learning to be patient with self. An important lesson I have learned is not to lose hope. Losing hope is like a death sentence. Without hope, it makes it difficult to pursue your goals, dreams, and to live life to the fullest. Feeling good about self is a process while dealing with life's trials and tribulations.

Currently, I am single. I hope to meet my better half someday. I don't want to have children, but would not mind getting married. In the meantime, I am learning to let go of past loves. I no longer chase after men. I rather wait for a man to pursue me in hopes that we will fall in love, and build a solid relationship with each other. I prefer to have a small circle of friends who care about me than an entourage of people who don't have my best interest at heart. I still have trust issues. As a result, I am more cautious in who I let into my life. I no longer hesitate to walk away from anyone who hurts me. I am not afraid to speak my mind, and I don't apologize for being honest. I do not conform to societal norms. I rather be true to myself.

I continue to struggle with depression. I try to stay focused on my goals and do things to lift my spirits. Writing this book is one of them. I did not know if I could write a book (writing blog posts are so much easier). Being able to express myself on paper gives me joy. I feel my words speak for me when I cannot verbally express how I feel. Yet, this story is more than my journey. It is a life's journey, I believe, many can relate to or have experienced. Through reflection, I have been able to identify, accept, embrace, cry, get angry, express, pray, write, and talk about all the things that affects me. I believe reflecting on one's life journey can be an effective way to understand self. It has for me. It is the reason I am still alive. I look forward to where this journey continues to take me, one reflective twist at a time.

Acknowledgements

My mom

My best friend, my partner in crime, no words can express how much I admire and love my mom. She is truly my rock and without her, I could not have done half of the things I am doing now. I admire her strength and appreciate her love for me. I thank her for always loving and supporting me.

My dad

I am his "mini me," because we are so much alike in many ways. I thank him for always encouraging me to stay focus and not give up on my dreams. I thank him for his love and always believing in me.

My bro, a fellow creative, has inspired me more than he may realize. His encouragement and love is what keeps me going. I thank him for believing in me and for not allowing me give up on myself.

My friend Gloria, who has been there for me when I was too embarrassed and stubborn to ask for help. I thank her for her friendship and love. It means so much to me.

My friend Tina, a fellow artist and longtime friend, I appreciate her for our many crafty-conversations, and exchange of art supplies and ideas, I thank her for being my friend and for the constant support.

I thank everyone who has been on this journey with me, on and offline. Thanks to all who reads my words. I hope my story inspires you. It is a joy sharing a part of my life with all of you.

References

Azar, B.S. (1996). Basic English Grammar. New York, NY: Pearson Education.

Collins, B. (2002). Nine Horses. New York, NY: Random House, Inc.

Deresiewicz, W. (2010). What are you going to do with that? The Chronicle of Higher Education. Retrieved from http://chronicle.com/article/What-Are-You-Going-to-Do-With/124651

Examiner.com (no longer available)

Foley, B.H., Pomann, H. (1982). Lifelines: Coping Skills in English. New York, NY: Pearson Education.

WPIX 11 news

YouTube.com/c/darakfulton

www.ingramcontent.com/pod-product-compliance
Lightning Source LLC
Chambersburg PA
CBHW051517120626
46551CB00012B/971